MAN GETS
SOBER

MAN GETS SOBER

*Men don't talk, so I wrote it down.
All the sh*t you need to get sober in one little book.*

Matthew Kerrison

Copyright © 2023 by Matthew Kerrison

All rights reserved. No part of this book may be reproduced or used in any manner without written permission of the copyright owner except for the use of quotations in a book review. For more information, please contact matt_kerrison@msn.com

First edition

Book & eBook Desing by Ravi R

This book is dedicated to Delphine, Oliver and Alice. I didn't do it for them, but without them I wouldn't have been able to do it for myself.

To my brother who showed me the way, as he has always done.

To Mum and Dad, I hope I've made you proud.

And to John for using up his spare time to read and reread this book. There were errors aplenty.

'No one can get sober for their jobs, for their wife, for their kids. They can't do it for any of that. They can only do it when they decide they're done.' Rob Lowe on THE KELLY CLARKSON SHOW

TABLE OF CONTENTS

1. Why Bother Reading This? 1
2. Dirty Washing 11
   The Cannabis Years 12
   The Ecstasy Years 17
   The Cocaine Years 22
   The Drinking Years 26
3. My Observations 31
   Kip 31
   Fatty Boom Boom 37
   The Fear of Missing Out 45
   Skint 53
   Boredom 59
   Rock Bottom Moment 62
   How to Help People With a Problem 70
   Health, But Who Gives a Shit? 79
   The Mental Problem 84
   Work 92
   Recovery 95
   Addiction isn't a Choice 98
   Loser 100
   We Are All Addicts 104
   How Do You Know if You Have a Problem? 107

4. Getting Sober 119
   Make Your Decision 119
   Decide if You Need Professional Help 122
   Create Your Plan 126
   Tell People (Or Not) 132
   Prepare Your Elevator Speech 135
   Do the Work 138
   Get Into Exercise 139

5. Staying Sober 147
   Slipping Up: The Fantasy of Using Again 147

6. Help Others 151
   What Good Has Come From Me Getting Sober 153
   Time to Recap... 155

CHAPTER 1
WHY BOTHER READING THIS?

If you're reading this book, chances are you're just like me – you fell in love with alcohol and drugs, or one or the other. You're also like me because you've gone past the point of fun and, whatever your drug of choice, it's starting to, or already has, fucked you up.

You'll notice I've used the word 'love'. That's because to get to the problem stage of drugs and alcohol, you will have adored it. At some stage, and quite likely for a long period of time, it will have been your love. Nothing better. Pure excitement and fun and you'll have valued it more than anything else you cared for.

True love.

I will state this now: there was nothing – and I mean nothing – I looked forward to more than the opportunity to drink alcohol and take drugs. My little combo was alcohol and cocaine and I absolutely loved them. They became my identity and gave me unbelievable times.

This may seem like a strange thing to do in the introduction of a book about getting sober – proclaim my love for the things that completely destroyed me – but I must be honest. The truth is, no one sets out wanting to be fucked up by alcohol and/or drugs. I had many happy times off my head and that is one of the hardest things about quitting, especially in the long run.

However, for me the fun became a habit and then an addiction or, put simply, the repetition of an act with no regard for the consequences.

If you're reading this book, then the effects of your habit are no doubt driving you (or have driven) you to the point where you know you need to stop and – more importantly – want to.

I'd lay money on the fact that deep down you know you're fucked and that you need to do something about it. The excuses have run dry, you've been caught out (again). You know damn well what people think about you, they have probably said things which will have really annoyed you, even though you know they're right. You're fed up with the regret, the embarrassment – you're possibly at rock bottom. Or not. It doesn't matter. But you know. You know it can't go on like this.

I don't care what anyone says, there's always a feeling inside saying, 'You're done, this fucking ends now.'

In short, the pain has arrived.

The pain is where it all starts. The pain that you so desperately want rid of.

It has outweighed the pleasure for some time now.

You know what you're doing is wrong and that only stopping will make things better.

Here's the first of the good news: stopping *will* make things better. I went through it. It immediately made *everything* better.

'The cure for addiction is suffering, you suffer enough, that something inside you goes, "I'm done".' Ben Affleck

In this book, I'll tell you how I gave it all up. I'll tell you without lying, without smoothing over the cracks, without fear for what my family will think when they read this.

This is a book about me, an everyday man who quit a serious alcohol and cocaine habit. What I did to get there, what I did when I was there, and ultimately what I did about it.

I promise, if you can use just two or three points from my story, it will help you to quit too. Anybody can change. They just need the tools and advice to guide them. Most importantly, they need to want to.

You're reading this book, so I know you want to change and simply by admitting that you're doing an incredibly brave thing.

This book is different. It will make you laugh; it will give you hope and it will be like looking in a mirror. It might not be one for two weeks in the Seychelles and no one's going to make a play out of this f*cker. But you will get a huge amount from it. The mere fact you're reading this is a great thing because it means that you've begun your journey. You've accepted you need help, to whatever extent that may be. And you're here, educating yourself for the biggest change in your adult life. Man, or Women.

I'll talk more about this later, so it may sound a bit wank now, but you should consider yourself a superhero. You're about to do something that many thousands of people can't do. You're about to stop drinking alcohol and/or taking drugs.

No cape required.

Before we really get started, a word on the title of this book. It was originally going to be called *A Normal Guy's Story of Problem Drinking, Drug Taking and What it Takes to Stop*.

However, I felt that there would be many people who would instantly have an opinion on this title and feel that because it had the word 'drugs' in it and they only had a problem with drink, the book wouldn't be relevant to them.

It is.

In fact, it really is time to forget the drink/drugs comparison. So many people seem to have less sympathy for those who take drugs, as opposed to those who drink.

Booze, in my opinion, is the worst.

The legal one. The marketed one. The one that can be bought everywhere. The one you have to apologise for not taking. The rite of passage. The one that can kill you. The one that can make you kill others. The one that cause you to lose your job. The one that can get you arrested. The one that takes hours away from your kids. The one that makes people beat the shit out of their wives or husbands. The one that can lead to rape … or was it? You'd had a lot to drink. The one that that causes more deaths than all other drugs combined.

But it's OK because you can buy it anywhere. It's legal. It's encouraged. It's socially acceptable. 'Go on, 'ave a drink!'

Whether you drink expensive French wine or cheap lager, it makes no difference. Booze gives zero fucks. So yeah, you might not associate yourself with a drug user in the typical sense, but I can assure you that that is irrelevant and this book can help. Even if it just makes you think then I've done my job. I made you think; not stare, not lose your underwear, but I made you think. And thinking is where it all begins.

So, what's this book going to do for you? What's it going to tell you? And more importantly, why the fuck should you listen to and take advice from a man who had problems with alcohol and drugs himself?

Well, the purpose is to make you take a good hard look at yourself and offer you some answers. They're out there; they work and can help.

I want to present you my thoughts on what 'having a problem' means and why it's no fucking surprise that millions of people have issues with drugs and alcohol.

I want to show you that there is a way out.

I want to give you hope and belief that life without booze and drugs isn't shit.

I want to help make you feel proud, because the chances are you haven't really felt proud for a long time.

If I can help any of you out there can get your life back on track and find the life you dream of when you wake up in the death throes of a hangover, full of regret and hatred, then I will have done a good thing.

I want to strip away what it's like to have problems with drink and drugs.

I want to get rid of the ridiculous stupid fucking stigma that society, and notably governments, have created about having alcohol and/or drug problems. When people give up smoking, everyone is full of encouragement, 'Well done, it's the best thing you've ever done!' 'Good choice man, those things will kill ya!' Yet when you tell people you've stopped drinking and taking drugs due to issues with them, they instantly paint you with a massive 'she/he is a fuckhead!' brush, have no idea what to say and often move quickly on in case you infect them or perhaps smell of piss.

I want to help show you that deciding to ditch all that shit doesn't turn you into a dull, Billy-no-mates with nothing to do but hanker after your former glory days, sitting in the misery of your own sadness for the rest of your life, waiting to die.

I'm not going to recommend veganism, meditation, holding hands with strangers or doing Joe Wicks workouts. But I am going to help you find other ways to spend your time, instead of getting fucked.

However, there is a caveat to all this. It is that you've got to believe me, and you've got to trust me.

Life can be good, really bloody good in fact. You don't need to be rich, you don't need to be successful, it doesn't matter what you look like – that's all bullshit. If you can get sober, you will restore pride in yourself and be able to say, 'I fucking did that.' Your life will change, I promise you.

The absolute touch is that it's free, it costs nothing. Not a sausage. And you will come out of the other side a fucking rockstar (a sober one).

Why Bother Reading This?

You'll also be unique. As I said before, you'll not do something that a huge percentage of the population do. You'll have said a big 'fuck you' to your problems, you'll feel the best you've *ever* felt, and you know what, being unique is fucking great. Be unique. Be fucking great.

I want to make it clear from the start that I'm not a doctor and none of what I'm going to say comes from medical journals. But then how many doctors have actually been through what the patient has? Doesn't that ever make you wonder? I'm not talking medically, but psychologically. After all, drug and alcohol problems are, in my opinion, mental health issues. It's about what's going on in your own head. Doctors can be the gateway to you getting help, but ultimately, it's your head and no doctor in the world can get inside it.

Please understand I'm not dissing doctors or suggesting you don't seek medical advice. There are countless cases where seeking a professional medical opinion is an excellent way to deal with alcohol and drug problems. But chances are they've never chugged vodka in the office toilets or snorted coke at their children's school play. They probably won't comprehend as to why someone would want to do that, or be able to share likeminded stories.

A doctor can give you guidance and it's a great place to start if you are seeking help. But really, truthfully, when you are about to make such a huge change as removing alcohol and drugs from your life, isn't it better to speak to people who have already done it?

There are some people who absolutely need the support of doctors as great danger is posed from simply stopping. For example, those who experience genuine withdrawal symptoms when not drinking, such as nausea, sweating, vomiting or even hallucinations. To those people, I ask you to read on, but of course seek the medical help you may need.

This book is aimed at what I call problem drinkers and drug takers. You know coming off this shit isn't going to kill you or put you in medical danger, but you admit you have a big issue. You don't get up in the morning necessarily needing a drink or drugs just to function, but you are probably thinking about what time you can start.

I can guarantee that I have gone through many of the same experiences, emotions, and mistakes as you. You may think that what you are going through is unique, but it's not. Millions of people are experiencing this pain, but only some want to change. And the fact that you're reading this means you want to change.

If this is the case, then I can help.

Here's a question. If you were going to attempt to jump between two buses on a motorbike, who would you listen to? The person who's spoken to lots of people who've done it, but has never actually ridden a motorbike themselves? Or the one who is covered in scars, with a body full of metal, but who has actually landed the jump?

Yeah, me too. And guess what – I'm the guy who made the jump.

I promise not to evangelise or go into any weird methods. Strangely, I don't have a hatred of drugs or alcohol. I believe anything in moderation is not a problem and many people can moderate. But ironically, those able to moderate don't need to think about moderation.

If you come to my home, there'll be alcohol on offer for those who would like it. Many people have the control required to allow them to drink it, so why shouldn't they? The same with drugs. If someone wants to snort coke in my house, fill your boots. I don't have any and won't take it, but please, be my guest.

The thing is, and this is an idea I'll develop further in this book, quitting any drug isn't about anyone else. Technically, unless you're in handcuffs or a padlocked gimp mask, the only person who can stop you drinking or taking drugs is you. I can give you advice, I can whisper shit in your ear, I can give you books to read, recommend group therapy, but I cannot be you.

Only you can do this. Not your friends, not your family, not your kids, not your doctor. Not me. You.

It's a simple choice: Are you going to stop or not? Not, 'I'd really like to stop', not 'stopping would be a good idea', not 'if only I could cut down'. No fucking good. There is no middle ground. If you're fucked and have made the decision that this needs to stop then you're halfway there.

'Recovery is not for people who need it, it's for people who want it.'
Anonymous

CHAPTER 2

DIRTY WASHING

I want to tell you a little bit about me.

This will do one of two things – either make you feel a lot better about yourself as your shit isn't nearly as bad as mine and you'll stop reading, or you'll feel that my problems weren't as bad as yours and you'll stop reading. Please don't. Drug or alcohol problems don't need to have a level of extremity to be passed off as genuine; I just want to share with you my journey through addiction and how it came to be. You'll know if you have a problem, and you wouldn't be here if you didn't. This isn't a competition.

The key thing about alcohol and drug problems is that they don't happen overnight. No one has ever had a line of cocaine and then gone, 'Right I'll have thirty grams of that please.' Same with booze, it's generally a very slow burner made worse by the fact that it's legal. It's the only drug in world you're actively encouraged to take. Even when you stop, people will still try to persuade you to 'have a drink!'

Strange that this doesn't happen when you give up smoking, another legal drug. Death by alcohol must clearly be the better option and is fully supported by friends, family and the government.

So here we go. If truth be told, my washing was pretty fucking clean for a long time. I started drinking at an average age; I was probably fifteen when I first tried alcohol and then seventeen when I began to consume it regularly. It was never my favourite drug, but don't discount the power it ended up having over me.

By the way, if drink is your only issue, please don't be put off by my foray into other recreational drugs. Alcohol held my hand throughout and then showed its true colours as I grew older. Stay with it, this book can still help you. In short, I'll be dealing with booze later.

Like most people, everything started when I was at school – drinking went from being a dare to becoming the weekend norm. But to be honest, at that time in my life booze wasn't the problem at all – the first drug I got really into was cannabis.

The Cannabis Years

'I used to smoke marijuana. But I'll tell you something: I would only smoke it in the late evening. Oh, occasionally the early evening, but usually the late evening – or the mid-evening. Just the early evening, mid-evening and late evening. Occasionally, early afternoon, early mid-afternoon, or perhaps the late-mid-afternoon. Oh, sometimes the early-mid-late-early morning ... But never at dusk!' Steve Martin

Fuck me, did I love cannabis. Cannabis turned a light on for me. Its effects were immediate the second you took a drag, and I loved the feeling it gave me. It didn't make you smell (well, apart from smelling of cigarettes, but you could get away with that in 1993). You could smoke it whilst driving (whilst still living at home, most of my spliff smoking took place in the car out of the prying eyes of my parents), no one could really tell that you were stoned and it was relatively cheap.

Cannabis became my thing and at the time I far preferred it to alcohol. You didn't get a hangover the next day, it was easy to get hold of and oh, that instant hit!

The one thing about cannabis that I refused to accept was that it was a gateway drug. I always used to think that the notion of a drug being a lead into other drugs was a nonsense. At the time I really didn't believe that there was a physical or psychological addiction to dope. I now look back and realise I was wrong. It certainly wasn't as strong as other drugs, but addicted I was. I smoked cannabis regularly for seven years. The good news is that when I stopped, I no longer went looking for it and it completely fell off my radar.

What it did do though was get me into trouble. Smoking hash in a car was practical, as I have mentioned, but it did provide the added risk of being caught by the police. A car of four young lads parked up is likely to attract attention and guess what? It did.

In 1993 I got caught by the fuzz. It happened to be the only time I had a significant amount of weed in my possession, approximately half an ounce. Sod's law I believe it's called.

It was the beginning of the summer holidays and I was working on the weekends to earn a bit of cash to spend during my time off. Fortunately (or unfortunately, depending on how you see it), the offer came up via a friend to buy a big fuck off bag of weed. My money was out in seconds.

Purchase made, I set off for a place to smoke it. That place was a friend's party. His parents were out and over I drove. Now at this point I'm going to add a comment which may put some people off. Please don't let it. I was not a rich kid, but my father was a business owner and that allowed us to have a comfortable life.

I was seventeen years old and drove a BMW 3 series. Yes. Done. Lucky fuck.

The car naturally attracted the attention of my friends and being the nice chap I am, I would let them drive it. That night I agreed to let one of my mates have a quick blast. There were four of us in the car and we rolled into a deserted car park. Or so I thought.

My mate hadn't been drinking, and I thought we'd be well hidden enough for him to have a spin. And spin he did. For the next five minutes he set about lighting up the rear wheels and handbrake turning the BMW around the car park. Loads of smoke, loads of laughter and loads of fun.

In fact, it was just the sort of fun you'd want to be having during your summer holiday when you're seventeen. Therefore, I think we thought a spliff would be the perfect thing to celebrate it. Sadly, the police didn't see things the same way.

The nearby residents weren't used to having a 'tyre fest' turn up in their village at ten at night, so one of them dialled 999 and the police turned up just as I was finishing off something that resembled an enormous traffic cone.

The bitch of the story is we nearly got away with it. In fact, if I hadn't shoved the rolling mat so hard under the driver's seat making the joint roll into the rear passenger's footwell, I don't think the police would have seen it and in turn wouldn't have searched the car.

But I did. And it did. And they did. And the half-ounce 'bounty' was quickly discovered.

I took the full blame. It was my weed, it was my car and my choices had led to that situation arising. My friends left on foot, I departed in the back of a police car.

To be honest it wasn't the arrest or in-depth interrogation that made it bad. It wasn't the chief of police screaming at me, it wasn't even being locked up that made it such a hideous ordeal.

It was the moment that three police officers told me that they were going to my house at two o'clock in the morning to search the place. It was then I knew I was fucked. Proper fucked.

As I remained in a cell, the police left to pay a visit to my address. There were no drugs in the house; I had told them that, it was the truth and indeed they didn't find anything. The killer was that I knew they were going to wake my parents – my mum and dad would find out and I was going to be in deep trouble.

I was released with just a caution, lucky boy. But going home at 3 a.m. to face my parents who were waiting for me in pyjamas and dressing gowns was the real punishment.

It's fair to say it wasn't pretty. The bollocking was, quite rightly, on another level.

This was the first time my addiction problems caused upset to my family, and sadly it wouldn't be the last.

And here's the thing. It changed nothing.

As I've said already, my simple definition of addiction is the continued repetition of an action regardless of the consequences. And it's the same for all drugs. If you're addicted and don't want to change, you'll keep going back. It really is that simple.

You could have defecated on the cake at your best friend's wedding, pissed on the vicar and dry humped the mother of the bride on the dance floor. You may have apologised in writing to every single guest for your actions, begged for forgiveness and made every excuse as to why these terrible events happened, but if you have a drink or drug problem and don't want to stop, you'll go back. You might swear that you'll never hit that level of degradation again, but you won't be able to guarantee that. You'll go back and make every excuse as to why going back is OK.

I carried on smoking cannabis until I was twenty-five, when I simply stopped. It wasn't a conscious decision, but my now wife moved in with me and wasn't into cannabis, so I stopped buying it and that was the end of that. Cannabis was a passage in time and I simply moved on.

I mentioned earlier that I never felt addicted to cannabis, never saw it as a problem. It has only recently popped back into my mind; since I got sober in fact. One of the reasons for this is something I'll go into more detail later, the 'fear of missing out'. The other cause was the irrational addict's realisation that if you stop drinking or taking drugs you're going to have nothing else to do, especially in social situations.

So when I eventually quit drinking, back came the thoughts of my old friend Mr Spliff. Now that I'm off the drink, what if I could just smoke weed? It was never a huge problem back in the day, I wouldn't be drinking, and I wouldn't be using Class A drugs. Yes, what a great idea!

Then I thought about it again and, fortunately for me, I saw sense. I knew if I went out and bought cannabis, I would go out and buy more and then some more and some more. Within a brief period, I would be back to smoking it every day.

In short, I would have simply shifted one problem to another. I know of people who've done this exact thing and it just doesn't work. If truth be told, it wasn't just the arrest that made cannabis a problem in my life. During my smoking days I failed my A levels (the exams you take at the end of secondary school in England, Wales and Northern Ireland), I hung out with many of the wrong crowd, became lazy, had no clear goals, and just wafted through eight years of my life. I disappointed myself and I knew that my family were no doubt aware that I was possibly at the beginning of a slippery slope.

So, I didn't buy any. Thank fuck.

The Ecstasy Years

'There's a guy in the place with a bittersweet face and he goes by the name of Ebeneezer Goode.' The Shamen

Unlike my parents who grew up in the rock and roll era of The Beatles, The Rolling Stones, Elvis, Cream and Bob Dylan, my formative years were during the dance era of Carl Cox, Paul Oakenfold, Daft Punk and Pete Tong. Born in the seventies, raised in the eighties, raved in the nineties.

I grew up just outside London and clubbing was everywhere. In 1993 I went to Club UK in Wandsworth and my life changed. I took a Dove, a Red Russian, reached for the lasers and literally went to heaven. For the next three years I took ecstasy every weekend.

I will say now, hands down, ecstasy is the best drug I have ever taken.

Whilst I don't recommend you go out and start taking Es, I do believe it's one of the most misunderstood drugs, especially from those who've never taken it. Certainly, for me at the time it didn't feel like it had the 'addictive' properties that I felt with other drugs. It really was a 'time and a place' type of drug and it had a purpose to it, namely clubbing. It wasn't like alcohol or cocaine that you could take at a dinner party, down the pub or in the toilets at work – though no doubt some of you may have done!

Pills, Es, Beans, Disco Biscuits, Scooby snacks or whatever you want to call them, were a real pleasure drug. I may not have got hooked on them in the manner of the other drugs I took, but that doesn't mean to say it was all plain sailing.

As with all drugs (and that includes alcohol, of course), they'll get you into trouble. During my ecstasy (and cannabis) years I was frankly a distant figure at school. Tiredness after the weekend's clubbing, coupled with the weed I was smoking daily, meant I had the attention span of a koi carp.

I had a Saturday job at a well-known supermarket and the early starts kept me out of trouble on Friday nights. Saturdays were my big night out, except for the rare times I wasn't working. One such occasion presented itself when I was at retake college. Retake college was where I'd been sent to redo my A Levels (Advanced level qualifications that can lead to university, further study, training, or work) that I'd completely failed at age eighteen. Most of my friends had passed them and headed to further education, but my drug habit had killed off any chance of that, as my attendance at school was so poor I failed every subject.

However, I wasn't stupid and quickly realised that I needed these qualifications as I too wanted to go to university. My parents kindly stumped up the money for me to spend a year relearning the work I'd missed and get the grades I needed. It worked, but that's not what this story is about.

As my final exams crept closer, it was announced that a revision session would be scheduled for a Saturday. This meant I wouldn't be able to go to work. Which meant I wouldn't have to get up at 5 a.m. Which meant I could go out on a Friday night for once.

The evening started with dinner at a restaurant with my parents. After our meal I asked if I could go and catch up with a friend for a drink or two. They said OK and off I went. On arrival at my friend's place I was greeted with a full-blown party. There were about thirty people there and within about ten minutes I had two Es in my hand.

I knew it was wrong, that it wasn't a good idea, but the brain of the addict comes up with every possible reason as to why this situation would be OK if I took the drugs, so take them I did – the continued repetition of an action regardless of the consequences.

I didn't make it home that night. In fact, I didn't make it home until the following evening. I'd stayed at that party for almost twenty-four hours.

I thought I'd been clever by phoning my parents at 9 a.m. saying that I'd slept at my friend's and would make my own way to school for the revision day. God knows how that conversation went; I dread to think of the state I was in when I spoke to my father.

Shortly after 11 a.m., my parents phoned the school and were informed that I hadn't turned up.

It will come as no surprise that my arrival at home that evening did not go well. It was almost certainly not helped by the smell of alcohol, my unwashed look, and the half-drunk bottle of wine I was carrying in a plastic bag. From the minute I walked through the door, I realised my parents knew.

It wasn't the telling off, it wasn't the fact that I had to confess to having lied to them, it wasn't even the state that I was in that etched this moment in my mind forever. No, it was the fact that my father cried. He cried because he was so disappointed in me. He cried because I was out of control and he knew there was nothing he could really do about it. My father rarely cries, but once again I had gravely disappointed him, and it broke me.

But as we all know, drugs don't give a fuck about this sort of thing. You would think it would have taught me a lesson. But it didn't.

Four weeks later I was arrested for drink driving.

'But you said alcohol wasn't a problem at that time?' I hear you say!

Technically, it wasn't. However, as many of you will know, alcohol is a useful tool following an ecstasy session to bring you down and give you the vague chance of sleep.

Having been out clubbing, I had headed to a friend's house and had a few drinks – not a huge amount – but enough for me to give a positive reading when the police pulled me over in my BMW at 3 a.m.

What an idiot. What the fuck was I doing in my car, high and slightly drunk at that time in the morning?

Well, at the time it all seemed so clear and obvious – we'd run out of cigarettes.

I had actually managed to buy the cigarettes and get back to my friend's house – I was stopped right outside.

I was very polite; I gave a positive reading but was allowed to wait another ten minutes to try again as my result was only just over the legal limit in the UK.

No good, I was still just over.

So off to court I went. With my parents.

It was horrendous.

They threw the book at me.

A twelve-month suspended license and a £1,000 fine. I was nineteen. It was 1995. My parents had to pay.

I thought things couldn't have been any worse.

Although they could have. Thank fuck it was 1995 and roadside drug testing was still fairly rudimentary.

They didn't test me for anything other than alcohol.

Nowadays, they would have been ticking a fair few things off the list.

Things did improve. I passed my exams and luckily for me I went to a university where ecstasy was difficult to get hold of and, more importantly, I didn't look for it, but this did nothing to halt my ascent into addiction.

The point is that whilst my stupid brain looks back fondly over my ecstasy years there were terrible downsides to it. I lost two years of my education, I wasted a huge amount of money, I know it had a detrimental effect on the relationship I was in at the time and most of all it caused my family terrible worry. The problem with me, alcohol and drugs was that I never just dabbled, it was all or nothing. I never associated this with the problems of addiction at the time, but with hindsight I know that's exactly what it was.

Sadly, despite a break of approximately three years where ecstasy and cannabis were no longer part of my life and my drinking was in no way a concern, a new drug came knocking on my door.

The Cocaine Years

'This year, more people will use cocaine than read a book to their children.' Michael Scott, The Office

I should really call this section the cocaine and alcohol years because where there's cocaine, there's always alcohol. No one just takes cocaine, they drink too. It's a devil of a partnership – when you drink, you get the urge to take cocaine and if you take coke, you want to have a drink. It's Laurel and Hardy, Mac and Cheese, Pooh and Piglet. I've tried just taking cocaine; it's horrendous, you simply must have a drink.

I don't remember the first time I took cocaine, and it wasn't really until I was working that I started to buy it on a regular basis. It's not cheap – approximately £40 for one gram which would last you for an evening out on most occasions.

At the beginning of my cocaine career, the cost didn't bother me too much as I managed to control my intake to once a week. For the first ten years it was a Friday night treat.

Stumbling across cocaine is very easy though. It's everywhere, and I mean absolutely everywhere. All cities are awash with it. I remember being in Milan with a friend once and we were heading back to our hotel after a night out at a club. Neither of us spoke a word of Italian, we'd never been to Milan before, but in the ten minutes it took to walk back to our hotel we had tested, negotiated, and bought a gram of cocaine. The only communication involved had been smiles, a straw, a thumbs up and €80. It was that easy.

I even scored a gram in Salt Lake City. The home of the Mormons in the bowl of the Wasatch Mountains where, at the time, bars and clubs were required to charge a cover, or a membership fee for foreigners to drink. That didn't stop me – I found a bar, became a member, met some people and two hours later was holding a small plastic bag with a Batman logo on it full of powder. Easy as pie.

Cocaine did it for me. The instant hit you get when you take it, the ability it gives you to party all night and drink like a fish without getting fall over drunk. At the beginning, it made me feel confident, horny, chatty – all whilst floating around in a fluffy bliss.

My problem with cocaine though, was that as soon as I could easily obtain it, it became my treat, my friend, the little bit of naughtiness that accompanied drinking so well. It was relatively discreet; you could take it pretty much anywhere and most of the time people wouldn't necessarily know you were on it.

I loved it for many years and truly felt it was under control. However, that all changed when it started to creep into the weekdays. It became something that, if I was going to have a drink, I couldn't be without. The issue here was that my drinking had also escalated, so if I knew I was going to have a drink in the evening then the chances were I would make sure I had some coke too.

This then started to encroach into the daytime, particularly on Fridays. It wasn't uncommon for me to start powdering my nose from 10 a.m. We'd go to the pub at midday for an hour or so, then I would carry on in the office until about 5 p.m. after which I would head home. Once at the house, it would be more wine and coke until about midnight. Effectively I would snort coke for approximately fifteen hours every Friday.

This went on for about a year until I got a new job in France. Truth be told, this was one of the reasons I was so happy to get this job as it meant getting away from cocaine. Going somewhere new to start afresh, reset, just be a drinker!

As many of you reading who have cocaine issues can probably already guess, this did not work. Cocaine is everywhere and within six months of being in France I had a new network of dealers. There I was, back at square one and putting my new life in jeopardy.

Apart from the obvious health-related effects, the bitch with cocaine is that it encourages you to make terrible decisions. Something that seems like a good idea when you're off your tits generally isn't. It got me into a lot of trouble. I would go out on weekends and not come home, I would sometimes lie about where I was, and I just became an incredibly selfish human being.

Cocaine became the most important thing in my life. I didn't really give a fuck about anything or anyone else as long as I had my fix.

It affected everything in my life. My relationships, my wealth, my health. Weekends were a mess, my work life was all over the place, but as long as I had a gram in my pocket none of that mattered.

It became my identity and I completely normalised it.

Now when I look back, I shudder with shame. Holding my children as babies with coke running down my nose, excusing myself from work meetings to take cocaine in the toilets, snorting it off the bins in my garden whilst pretending I was just going outside for a cigarette, taking coke in my parent's house, even doing it in the toilets of my kids' school whilst waiting for a parent-teacher meeting. I was out of control, a mess. But I totally normalised it. For me, it was OK and the only fear was getting caught.

However, things changed once my family joined me in France, I knew the game would soon be up. I didn't have the social life we had before, hiding it was getting increasingly difficult and frankly I'd had enough.

There was only one way it would stop. I had to cut off the supply. It had to become impossible for me to get hold of cocaine. When I first arrived in France there had been a six-month period without it, and this hadn't been a problem. The dealers had to go, the numbers in my phone erased for good. If I couldn't buy it, I couldn't take it.

Luck then came my way, though at the time I didn't see it that way. The two dealers I knew disappeared. They didn't answer their phones and never contacted me again. This was my chance. I made a pact with myself that I would not seek out any other dealers, I would not speak to anyone to see if they knew someone who could 'sort me out'. I knew this was the only way.

It worked. Without the supply, I could not partake.

A strange thing happened about a year after I got fully sober – I saw one of those dealers walking down the street. I didn't speak to him, things had changed, but I know how the conversation would have gone twelve months earlier. I didn't approach him, but I did consider it. I wanted to thank him for disappearing. Had he not, I may never have stopped.

Unfortunately, giving up cocaine was not the end of my problems.

The Drinking Years

'When success happened to me, there wasn't a day that went by when I didn't have a drink. I'd be topping up all the time. I could fall asleep on a plane before it took off and wake up to the sound of 100 miniature bottles of vodka clicking together. The only thing that would be left in my mini bar was the fucking Toblerone.' Marti Pellow

I drank from the age of fifteen to forty-four. Twenty-nine years of boozing. I drank at least two to three times a week during the first twenty-five years and then really got into my stride for the last four. I never considered myself to be an alcoholic, but then what is the definition of an alcoholic? Many say it is someone who has the inability to stop drinking despite potential or actual negative consequences. Well, if that's the definition then I guess I was, and so must millions of people be around the world. But of course, they, like me, do not class themselves as alcoholics.

How many people do you know who could, as of right now, not have a drink for the next two weeks? I am not talking physically, but how many people would after a day or two be thinking about alcohol and pissed off that they couldn't have a drink because they'd said they wouldn't. Many would crack, fuck it off and come out with something like, 'I've nothing to prove, I'm an adult, I'm not an alcoholic, if I want to have a drink, I will.'

I bet numerous people would struggle to do this and yet we wouldn't class them as alcoholics. So what is it, if not addiction? That need, desire to have a drink even if they've said they wouldn't.

This is a massive grey area and one I fell firmly into. The problem with the word 'alcoholic' is that we associate it with the worst of the worst, the dregs of society – as a middle-class man with a job, wife, kids, a nice home and great friends it couldn't possibly apply to me.

But the reality was that, by pure definition, I *was* an alcoholic. I could not go, or should I say didn't want to go, more than a day or two without a drink. I will talk more about this later, but I think the word 'alcoholic' is such a difficult one, I believe that it's stopping many people seeking help as they don't want to have this label put on them. I therefore refer to myself as a problem drinker and that's what many of us are, problem drinkers.

I drank relatively normally for many years. The change really happened when I had kids and went from drinking at the pub at the weekend to boozing at home. Everything changes when you drink at home: it's cheaper, you control the measures and you can do it on your own without judgement.

Wine was my thing and fuck me did I love red wine. It was never a glass though, always a bottle, regardless of what day of the week it was. If I opened a bottle, I would always finish it.

In the evening, drinking was the only thing I really wanted to do. I always used to pride myself on the fact that I didn't watch much TV, but the reason for that was that I was too busy getting pissed. I was also good at drink 'pushing'. I knew that if my wife had a drink or two, she would relax and I'd be able to drink more. It's fair to say that I was the best host in the world, forever filling up her glass so I could take advantage of her lowered defenses and open that prized second bottle. Cunning little cunt I was.

The problem with drink is that it creeps up on you. It's unusual for people to start abusing it quickly; it generally takes many years, and this was certainly my case. In the end I found myself thinking about booze every day, even if I didn't necessarily drink it. Waking up in the morning after a night off drinking, I would already be wondering how I would be able to have a drink that evening because I didn't have one yesterday. I would look for any excuse.

The situation started to escalate when the control disappeared. When I got the job in France, my kids were in school in the UK and it was too much of a risk to move the whole family out straight away in case things didn't work out with this company. It was a fresh start but whilst I wanted to use it as a springboard to start a new life and stop drink and drugs, it actually had the opposite effect.

I ended up spending eight months on my own in Paris. I returned to the UK most weekends, but for the majority of the time it was just me, work and my apartment. I managed to control my drinking to a certain extent as I genuinely didn't want to fuck things up workwise, but I did drink almost every night and in many ways my habit escalated. I'd get home, not have much else to do, so wine it would be.

My family eventually moved out with me, but the drinking didn't stop.

On occasion, I would drink during the day, mainly at a work lunch, but whilst my colleagues would happily stop at 2 p.m. I would want to carry on. Work was fairly social so I could get away with it, but there were times when I was coming home from a day in the office almost drunk. It crept up on me, I knew it was wrong, but I kept doing it.

There are – and I will be going into – the more obvious adverse effects booze has on sleep, money and quality of life, both mentally and physically. But there was one particular occasion that properly shocked me. And still does to this day.

It was much ado about nothing really. One day I was invited to a BBQ by my best friend over here in France, and I did something I'd never done before – I became aggressive. It was a silly situation, but he'd been given some food that turned out to be spicy and it made him feel sick. He, like I, was drunk and he gave his wife a mouthful suggesting that it was her fault that he had it on his plate.

With a head full of alcohol, I took offence to this and stood up and started shouting at him. I was full of anger and aggression, and here I was squaring up to my mate because of a flippant comment he'd made that didn't even concern me. It came to nothing, but I felt deeply ashamed of my behaviour. I often think it's a pity the moment wasn't captured on film, so I could see for myself just what an absolute dick I'd been, all because I was drunk.

Drink in the end just wasn't working for me – I couldn't control it. There was no moderation, and it was the only thing I wanted to do in my spare time. It robbed me of many things – time with my children, job progression, relationships – and life just went by in a haze from session to session. I will talk about this more in a later chapter, but it all came to a head on 10th May 2019. I had my rock bottom moment. The moment when I knew the game was up. On that day, everything changed.

It was the day I decided I needed to change and there was only one thing blocking that change from happening: alcohol.

I have not had a drink, or any other drug for that matter, since.

CHAPTER 3
MY OBSERVATIONS

In this chapter I want to share with you all the things I noticed when I stopped drinking and taking drugs. As an addict there is so much you ignore, when you get sober you see it all for how it really is.

Kip

Not long ago I attended an hour-long 'lunch and learn' session at work. There was no lunch and to be honest, I didn't learn much, but the topic was of interest to me.

'Sleep – the key element to wellbeing.'

It was basically a hippy bollocks workshops about twenty-four-hour cycles, the roles of melatonin, tryptophan (look it up), the pineal gland (it's not your cock), not eating meat at night and the theory that shredded carrots can apparently help you sleep. Go figure.

However, at no point did they discuss the effects of alcohol on sleep.

Let me make this clear: alcohol fucks with your sleep, big time. It's the side effect that all drinkers ignore or seem to dismiss as unimportant. I'm not talking about when you've had a few, or a lot, and you fall very quickly into a deep sleep, but that 4 a.m. period when it wakes you up.

I can tell you this for a fact – since stopping drinking, I sleep like a king. The difference is incredible. I cannot emphasise how much of a difference it has made. The reality is that even a couple of glasses of wine can affect your *sommeil* (fancy French word for sleep).

Be honest, if you drink, how many times have you woken in the night and started worrying about shit? Money, relationships, work problems. You go to bed tired, wake up tired and fumble through the day like a zombie cunt.

When I was drinking, I forgot what real sleep was. I really did. I thought I'd had a good night's sleep but hadn't.

Here's the sciencey bit as to why. There is no doubt that drinking booze often reduces the time it takes to fall asleep. It is, after all, ethanol (or C_2H_6O). For those of you who are unaware ethanol, or alcohol, is a volatile, flammable, colourless liquid with a slight odour. It is a known psychoactive substance, recreational drug and the active ingredient in alcoholic drinks. Boom, I'll have some of that then!

Another interesting fact is that the largest single use of ethanol is in your car. It is used as fuel and a fuel additive, and it is particularly popular in Brazil due to it's sugarcane based ethanol fuel programme. Brazil is in fact a biofuel industry leader and has been for the past forty years. It is also used to make solvents.

The way alcohol works is pretty straightforward – it depresses the central nervous system and has a sedative effect that helps you relax and makes you drowsy, so essentially you fall asleep faster.

This sounds like a good thing, right? A wonder drug! Why can't we give booze to babies? I was tempted many times with mine (that's not actually true, before you sling me in front of social services).

Here's where it all goes tits up. Once you've done some drinking and gone to bed, your body concentrates on getting rid of all the booze. Alcohol is a diuretic (it makes you pee a lot) and as your body starts cracking through whatever you've tipped down your gullet, it has to work super hard to metabolise it. This has three effects.

Firstly, you wake up desperate for a piss, or you don't wake up and you pee on your girlfriend. True story, but this was no golden shower and yes, before you ask, I slept in the wet patch. In short, your metabolism has created a ton of urine and you need to get rid of it.

Secondly, your body is as dry as a camel's arsehole. Due to the diuretic delights of booze, you tend to urinate a huge amount and are then presented with a hangover. A hangover is essentially dehydration, your body screaming out for fluids.

Finally, and this one's the real fucker, there's what is commonly termed as 'the rebound effect'. Your body is so fucking delighted that it's dealt with the depressant effect of alcohol that it gives you a little boost of adrenaline which wakes you up. 'Right, you cunt! I'm done with sorting out this shit you've put in me, now you can wake up and have a good old fucking worry about everything!' Hello, anxiety!

This adrenaline can also create a scary racing heartbeat. I can remember occasions when I have woken up with my ticker going ten to the dozen, it felt like it was going to explode out of my chest.

Be honest, how many of you have woken up with these symptoms? Heart thumping away, desperately needing a wee but can't be fucked to get out of bed and wishing you had water. *La totale*, the whole kit and caboodle. Then, to top it off, you start shitting yourself about tomorrow's PowerPoint slides that you should probably have finished before you left the office, but you decided to go out and get smashed instead. Now it's 4 a.m. and you're awake and you're fucked. Consumed with worry, panic and yet more worry.

The one thing I did take from the lunch and learn session was that this second half of the night is the time you should normally be experiencing REM.

No, not listening to 'Shiny Happy People', but Rapid Eye Movement.

This is the part of sleep where you dream. Where your brain runs wild. Whether you're getting jiggy with Scarlett Johansson, scoring the winning goal in the World Cup or maybe trying on your Auntie Dawn's bras, this is a key part of sleep. This is where REM occurs. So what?

Well, according to the National Institute of Neurological Disorders and Stroke, a study depriving rats of REM sleep significantly shortened their life span from two or three years, to just five weeks. Rats deprived of all sleep cycles lived only three weeks. The importance of REM is attributed to the fact that during this phase, your brain exercises important neural connections which are key to mental and overall wellbeing and health.

Now, you're probably not a rat and you haven't been deprived of all sleep cycles (unless you're on coke – I'll come to that). However, missing out on REM can worsen daytime sleepiness – that's why you're likely to feel much less alert and the day drags after a night of drinking.

In short, booze fucks with your sleep. When you stop, it changes. The difference is simply monumental. I can assure you. I know.

Drugs don't help either. For approximately fifteen years I didn't sleep on Friday nights, or not really anyway. Being smashed on booze and coke there would be many Saturday mornings that would just simply arrive. Sleep was nigh on impossible, I would lie in bed for six hours, mostly thinking of porn and waiting (dreading) for morning to arrive.

When I look back, I simply do not know how I coped. I felt like shit most weekend mornings. I remember snorting coke and sneaking swigs of booze throughout Saturday mornings in a vague attempt to stay fucked and function. I took my kids to French lessons, praying no one would talk to me in case they smelt the alcohol on my breath. Though if that were to happen, I would simply laugh it off and blame my booze breath on a 'party' the night before and just, well, function.

And function I would. And function many of us do. That's what makes it so hard. You keep up the façade, you go through the motions, counting down the time until you can have your next drink or line – 7 p.m., 6 p.m., 5 p.m., maybe lunchtime if you're lucky.

Something that has always amused me is that many problem drinkers try and convince themselves that they don't have a problem, purely based on what time they have their first drink. The famous booze o'clock.

How many problem drinkers hide behind this concept? Many.

The whole idea that just because you only drink after 6 p.m. means you don't have an issue is simply ludicrous. I know quite a few people who stick to booze o'clock but will then polish off a bottle of wine or two every day once that clock strikes six. Clearly though, because they only drink in the evening, they don't have a problem. I think that's fucked-up logic.

In fact, let's be honest, this sense of there being a morally correct time for drinking fuels the bullshit that shields some drinkers from admitting that they have a problem. I know as I used this reasoning all the time.

I would generally only ever drink in the evenings, and only if I had been on a drug binge and was still fucked would I consume a drink before lunchtime.

I genuinely convinced myself that I did not have a problem as I would only drink in the evening and not every day.

When you do drink too much, you also become quite defensive, often stating categorically that you don't drink every day and never during the day. It's your immediate defense when people may suggest you are a heavy drinker.

The reality for me was that I often wouldn't want to drink in the day, or every day, because I'd still be feeling so fucking wank after drinking the night before. That was often the only thing that kept me off the drink and drugs, feeling too shit to want to do it.

There would often be times when the evening would come around and that first drink would be quite unenjoyable, unpleasant even. But down it would go and then the devil would be back on your shoulder ... have a few more ... buy some coke.

Then you don't sleep, then you're tired (even though you pretend not to be) and the cycle begins again.

So many people I know who drink, and not necessarily to excess, have sleep problems.

If you take drugs, you know why, but for those who just booze, almost none of them are willing to entertain the fact that it's due to the alcohol they drink.

It's not complicated: stop drinking and you'll sleep better. It really is one of the most wonderful results of getting off the booze. That alone changes your life.

Fatty Boom Boom

Right, I'll apologise now if you find this offensive. But if you do, please fuck off.

Booze makes you fat. And if you keep drinking alcohol whilst trying to lose weight, it will never work, and you'll always be fat.

Got it?

I should really just stop here as it's that simple. Stop drinking and I can pretty much *guarantee* you will lose weight.

This might seem like fat shaming, but I can say it because I was a bit on the large side myself. How many fat fucks have I seen (me included) waste money on gyms, eat salad at work, buy those 'count on us' ready meals, only to remain the size of a fucking whale.

And here's what I guarantee. None of them – not one – will have tried removing alcohol from their diet.

Because alcohol could never be the cause, and we all need a bit of a release now and then, a bit of what you fancy. You know what I mean ... don't you, fatty!

I kept my decision to quit drinking quiet at the beginning (another topic for later), but even the people who didn't know or who I hadn't told noticed something had changed. Why? Because the weight fell off me. And you know what? It felt fucking great.

In one year, I lost fifteen kilograms. I wasn't even trying to lose weight, or at least not intentionally. It simply fell off when I stopped drinking alcohol.

What's more interesting is that for many years I have loved running. I even ran the London Marathon in 2011 (no Speedy Gonzales, just under five hours, but I was chuffed as fuck just to finish). I even managed to keep it up throughout my heavy drinking and powder days.

I wasn't in any way efficient, it was often hard work and, on some occasions, I would still be pissed whilst jogging (yes, it is possible). To be honest, I just about continued and ran at least once or twice a week despite being mostly off my tits.

Here's the thing. I lost no weight. In fact, I put weight on. Pummelling my way up to a tubby ninety-five kilos. I can remember on several occasions catching sight of my gut whilst putting on my socks next to a mirror and thinking that I'd frankly become an enormous blancmange. I could however, when standing, still see my cock, just. Always a good way for a man to judge just how fat he has become. I'm sure many men lost sight of their gentleman sausage years ago.

So, what about it? People say there's no magic bullet to weight loss. I am telling you that if you drink too much then for numerous cases there is. Many people, including me, are living proof that for both women and men, when you knock the booze on the head, you lose weight, gain confidence, have more energy and, for us gents, get to see your willy a lot more. Happy fucking days!

I think that this message should be pushed. I believe that doctors, weight counsellors, gym instructors and dietitians need to put stopping drinking at the top of the agenda for those who genuinely want to lose weight. If you are serious about losing weight, stop drinking. Because if you stop drinking, you will lose weight. Simple.

It also proved to be a massive motivation for me to stay off alcohol. When you see the weight go, you feel proud. Pride in yourself is truly one of the biggest rewards you get when you quit drink or drugs.

That 'I've fucking done this!' feeling. It's the best.

Now that is not to say that the desire won't come back, because it will, big time and probably often. In fact, I would argue that it will never really leave you, but, like an ex-partner, eventually it will take the hint, fuck off and stop bothering you so much.

The pleasure I got from losing weight and looking like the old me was a big thing. And so it should be. It's a noticeable side effect and you get the nicest compliments about it. Especially enjoyable when they're from your wife's friends. The hot ones.

Another 'cheeky bonus' was my blood pressure.

I'd always kind of ignored my blood pressure, put it to the back of my mind and thought that my twice weekly jog would allow me to get away with it.

However, I had seen more and more of my overweight and drinking pals find out that they had high or 'highish' blood pressure. 'No problem,' they would say, 'I have tablets that control it, I take one a day and carry on as before.'

My view was different, I thought, 'Fuck that!'

When I moved to Paris, I had to have a medical at my new job. This is normal in France; employers there insist you have one every two years. It's pretty straightforward – it involves measuring your height, your weight, asking questions such as do you like cigarettes (no mention of booze, unsurprisingly), have you got any current medical conditions and finally a blood pressure test.

The results of my first medical were just about OK – I had tried to take the booze and coke down a notch as I wanted to be relatively efficient in my new role and make a half decent impression.

Once the second examination came around two years later, I'd had time to settle, smash a lot of alcohol and found myself a small army of cocaine dealers.

My blood pressure was high. Not bad, but on the high side. I was told to come back in a month for it to be retested.

Fortunately or not, depending on how you look at things, this coincided with my 'rock bottom' moment and my eventual decision to get sober. In fact the medical took place only a short time afterwards.

When I went returned, I hadn't touched booze for three weeks and not sniffed even a wafer-thin line of coke in well over two months.

The first thing the doctor noticed was that I'd already lost four kilos. Next, my blood pressure was completely back to normal.

She congratulated me and I tap danced out of there like Gene Kelly with an umbrella. Fucking chuffed, fucking proud.

So why does booze make you a fat cunt?

First up, it's packed with calories. If, for example, you drink a bottle of wine per day, that's approximately 600 calories (more for stronger wine). That's roughly the equivalent of thirteen Jaffa cakes, three Mars Bars or twenty-eight Jelly Babies … per day. To burn this off you would need to run for about six miles or ten kilometers.

If an ale is your tipple of choice, a pint of beer is approximately 240 calories. Three chocolate digestives for you right there. To get rid of this, that's a thirty-minute swim.

So if you smash a bottle of wine every night, you're looking at 4,200 calories a week. A forty-two mile run or pretty much a nine hour swim.

None of this is meant to be scientific or exact, but to give you an idea, the average daily recommended calorie intakes for men and women are as follows: 2,500 for a bloke and 2,000 for a woman.

Which means if you are drinking a bottle of wine a day (or not quite a whole bottle per day but smashing it on the weekends) you are adding an extra two days' worth of calories every week. That's 104 days of extra calories a year – 218,400 calories, or 397 Big Macs.

Wondering why your arse is wider than your shoulders? Or why you've grown a beard to hide that extra chin? Look no further.

As a side note, and I used to kid myself about this too, I love it when blokes happily say they are only a thirty-four-inch waist when there's a tsunami of gut cascading over the top of their jeans. Nice look that.

The other pisser about all this is that booze calories are so-called empty calories.

What does this mean?

Basically, when you drink booze and then eat, the body burns the alcohol first. So, for example, if you've been out on the beers and then devour a KFC, your body will burn the drink calories before the food and this means the KFC is much more likely to be stored as fat. Bargain Bucket Boobs.

This is why trying to lose weight when you're still on the sauce is so difficult, because whatever you eat is going to be stored as fat as your body breaks down the booze first. The sheer volume of calories in alcohol means that it's an uphill battle if you want to shed some pounds.

I know so many people who almost starve themselves, but just won't have it that drink is the issue. One of my favourites was from my friend's wife who, on seeing my dramatic post-pisshead weight loss, defended her husband's massive gut by saying that he is not made up of the same morphology as me.

Utter bollocks. I have pictures of the two of us in our twenties; he was arguably slimmer than me. Now he drinks every day.

This brings me on to another thing which fucks you up. An enzyme called Aldh1a1.

This little fella is responsible for converting alcohol to fat, particularly around the Derby Kelly (belly) and organs. He is also age aware, especially for women, and knocks on your door big time post-menopause.

Ladies, this is what can cause your middle-age spare tyre when oestrogen levels fall as the menopause approaches. Sorry to add even more depression to what can already be a tricky time!

But lads, don't think we get away with this. Oestrogen production suppresses this enzyme, and we don't produce anything like the levels that women do. Hence, it's with us all the time.

This also, in my view, coincides with the wrong time in life – our forties and fifties. Many people are now at that stage when we're earning enough money to live on, and we no longer have babies to look after.

This is when many people start drinking at home. You no longer associate booze with going out as you did in your twenties and thirties, now you're at home controlling the flow of your own grog.

And let's be honest, your glass of wine at home is in no way measured and is, more often than not, fucking massive.

When you're middle aged and at home boozing whenever you want, effectively everything is against you. It's beer bellies and wine waists all round.

The next issue is stuffing your cake hole.

Whether it be an evening with crisps, dips, olives, saucisson and various other snacky shit that's served up during pre-dinner drinks, or the infamous problem of the munchies the next day – 'If I don't have McDonald's now, I may actually die' – booze not only makes you eat more, but it also means you do not give a flying fuck about what you eat.

Let's face it, when you've had a skinful, no one staggers into the kitchen the next morning, head pounding, pants half wedged up their arse and asks if there's any leftover humous and carrots.

According to a BBC report, alcohol switches the brain into starvation mode, increasing hunger and appetite.

In tests on mice, alcohol activated the brain signals that tell the body to eat more food. Can't be all bad being a lab mouse, I hear you say.

However, for us humans, it makes us fat. I experienced it, I see my friends do it. They try repeatedly to diet and lose weight, but they are still the size of a house. The weekends are the worst. People will fight through the week surviving on the diet of a fussy three-year-old, only to hit the bottle on Friday, Saturday and Sunday and eat whatever the fuck they want. Cheese trolley? Wheel it over here, my friend.

The other thing that many people tend to ignore is that booze makes you a lazy cunt.

Cannot. Be. Fucked.

Those words are a pretty apt description of my Saturday and Sunday mornings, or afternoons, following a boozing (and/or drug) session. I had the motivation of a potato and frankly all I wanted to do was sit on my arse and wait until I felt slightly better so that I could drink some more.

That's a slight lie – I did sometimes find motivation, but that was mainly based around making something to eat. When I say 'making', I mean shuffling from the sofa to the fridge, grabbing something edible and then resuming my position doing fuck all. Occasionally, I'd get up and go shopping, super motivated. Look at me, I'm off out on a Saturday morning to the shops, to buy food! Then I'd get to the drinks aisle. Hit 'replay' please.

So here you have it. Booze makes you fat. End of lesson.

The Fear of Missing Out

The fear of missing out (FOMO for short, although I hate acronyms) is all about how the fuck am I going to cope when everyone else is getting smashed and I can no longer do so.

There's no doubt about it, this is probably the hardest thing to deal with when getting sober. And what makes it a real bitch is it tends to come on really strong once you've sorted yourself out for a while.

It's a bit like an ex-partner; it can come back out of nowhere and on occasions of weakness, you might think about having a little go again.

It's the reminiscing that really slaps you about with FOMO. After a while you start to forget about the fucking horrific, self-destructive, chaotic, 'off your tits' lifestyle that drink and/or drugs created. You start to remember the good times, the fun, the adventure, the excitement. This generally happens when you're bored or in situations that you formerly associated with your habit.

My Friday nights used to go as follows:

Leave work, very excited that it's the weekend.

Drive towards home.

Phone my drug dealer approximately fifteen minutes before I wanted to score.

Meet, pick up some coke.

Drive to the supermarket.

Snort coke in the toilets of the supermarket.

Float around the supermarket buying food (not that I wanted it, as eating when you're coked up is a frankly Herculean effort. Cocaine massively suppresses your appetite and causes you to almost gag when eating. It's very tricky, believe you me. Every tried eating cardboard? Do half a gram of coke and sit down for dinner – you'll see.)

Buy a bucket load of booze in the supermarket.

Drive home.

Get drinking.

And you know what? For a long time, when my habit felt semi under control, I absolutely fucking loved doing this. No doubt about it, it seemed like the best thing in my life. Those Friday nights when everything came together and I was high and drunk in my nice kitchen, I was in a place of fucking joy. Or so I believed.

The reality was, I was simply lying to myself. On the coke side of things, it had to be done in the utmost secrecy. My wife could not know. This meant hiding in the toilets, our bedroom, even the shed. It involved covering my tracks, not sleeping and occasionally getting up in the night to drink booze. I never hid booze but I often wished I had done. In my mind I always held the thought that concealing alcohol was a step too far, but I never really needed to as there was always plenty in the house and most of my drinking was done during so-called 'acceptable hours'.

When you get sober, you look back with embarrassment. You realise that this was not normal behaviour. Yes, I felt like I had some control, but I didn't really. That is addiction.

However, here's the difficult bit – once you get sober, your stupid fucking brain often likes to remind you of the pleasure, not the pain. It likes you to remember only the good times.

Your thoughts will start to take you back to the happy place. Remind you that now you are missing out. All that fun stuff has gone. Those great nights you had, the fun chaos that ensued, the times when your addiction seemed under control (although if you're honest with yourself, it never was) ... You remember having had such an amazing time.

You'll also feel bitter and angry. Not with anyone else, but with yourself. You will experience thoughts such as, 'Why couldn't I control it? Why did I have to be the one that couldn't just slow down or moderate? Why am I now missing out?'

For me, this really kicked in after the six-month stage. By this point you've done the hard bit. You've stopped. You've proved to everyone that you can do it and that you've changed, which you no doubt have.

But I guarantee the fear of missing out will creep into your head. What makes it worse is you'll start to rethink your problem; in fact you'll begin to think that maybe you didn't really have a problem. After all, you've not touched drink or drugs for six months and it wasn't that difficult.

This is where you are in real trouble. Trust me, I know.

I gave up for about eight weeks four months before I fully stopped.

Cured. Obviously not a problem for me. I can stop at the drop of the hat. None of my mates quit, but I did. I can now control my drinking. I will never go back to how it was before. I don't have a problem anymore. Well done me!

Sadly, as I discovered, this was utter bullshit. A utopian dream addicts will happily grab on to so they can again taste the poison that once ruined them.

Within a week I had scored more cocaine, stocked up on booze and was back to pre-quitting levels. I got right back into it.

The fear of missing out can be evil and you've got to be aware of this little cunt.

Parties and holidays can be a particular problem. I found parties less difficult to deal with as I just stopped going. But I would never say no to a holiday.

For me, holidays were basically an opportunity to drink in the sunshine for a week or two. I never did drugs on holiday. I didn't feel the need to risk taking them with me and for some strange reason, maybe because we were all together as a family, I just didn't think it felt right or necessary.

Alcohol though, I did. And I loved it.

The main reason was that I could get away with drinking at lunchtime *and* in the evening, or sometimes from lunchtime *until* the evening and beyond.

We always holiday with friends or family and often club together for a villa with a pool. Whilst this was genuinely done for reasons of space, your own place and fun for the kids, it was also a great excuse to drink like a fish every day.

The classic line to the children would be, 'We're going to stay at the villa today, we've paid for it so want to make the most of it.' Which basically translated to, 'Us adults will be drinking all day and therefore be too fucked to drive anywhere, or indeed be too fucked to do anything with you kids ... Now go and get your swimming costumes on and yes, you can sit on the iPad all day.'

Whilst both the kids and adults always had a good time, there was a selfishness about it.

Holidays were an absolute blast with booze flowing all day, late lunches, and long siestas. Ah, how I reminisce!

And so it gets you again. The fear of missing out. When I go on holiday in the future, I will no longer be able to do that again. Or maybe I will? Just on holiday, that would be OK wouldn't it?

No. It won't. I know it won't and so do you.

The reality is, you *can* have great holidays when you give up drinking. They're different, yes, but there is so much you can do. I'll be telling you more about this in the chapter 'Getting Sober', but be aware, the holiday booze monkey will come and tickle your ear from time to time. You have to have a plan.

As for parties, I think it depends on how old you are when you ditch the drink or drugs as to the effect this has. If you're young, then it is likely to be harder. Parties and going out are your social lifeline, and it will be tough if you decide to attend them sober. However, once you are there, you quickly realise that unless they're with a close group of friends, they are a tiresome affair. Here's a little insight into how the old me used to deal with them. I'm sure this will resonate with many of you.

I would always make sure I arrived at a party semi-fucked. I would always have two or three drinks before going out, even if just for dinner. If I had coke on me, I would have at least two to three lines before turning up.

The reasons for this were as follows. I never knew how much booze would be on offer at a party. In France, where I have now been living for four years, the *apéritif* (fancy word for pre-dinner drinks, or just drinks), would often be a very controlled situation. Your host would regulate the flow of alcohol usually having it in another room or on another table. This, for a problem drinker, is a fucking nightmare; sipping is simply not an option.

Also, you are entirely dependent on the speed at which other people drink. When you love booze, this is *never* fast enough. This can also be true at a pub or bar. You can't go and get another round when your mate's wife is constantly talking and has barely touched her half a cider.

This leads to sneaky behaviour. If I headed up to fetch a round on my own, I might sneak in a double whisky at the bar, make up for lost time. If I had coke in my pocket, regular trips to and from the toilets would occur.

At a party or in a bar, you want access to alcohol, and easily. My second and very simple trick would be to take a lot of booze to a party. This would allow you to pressure the host into opening more, or even better, allow you to open it and sort out some proper dosage.

'We must try that Montagny Premier Cru that I bought, it's a gem! No, no, you sit down, you've done enough today

– I'll sort these drinks out!' Cue massive glasses of wine for everyone and at least two bottles opened and plonked in front of the group (though clearly nearest to me …)

Be honest with yourselves, how many of you are reading this and know damn well that you also do these things? Many of you, I'm sure.

It's the same with restaurants. One bottle? No, order two straight away. That way you know that you can tuck in and quickly. Sometimes I would barely be seated before I was beckoning the waiter over. Arms waiving above my head like I was trying to land a plane, just to get the drinks order in before there was any faffing about.

Me on booze and coke, chatting at a party, was no doubt a dull affair for anyone other than myself. I had all the answers, I was a business guru, great looking, women loved me and fuck me I was witty! I thought I was the bollocks, mega popular, the life and soul. Mr Fucking Party.

I was not. I subsequently found out that some of the people I thought I was close to actually held things against me. I would leer at their girlfriends or wives, I was somewhat chaotic, and they saw me for what I really was; a heavy-drinking cokehead.

I actually found this out when I was still drinking and taking drugs. The revelations hurt but my reaction was one of defiance. 'After all I've done for them! Look at me living in Paris with a great job – they can fuck off!' All the pretentious shite I was full of.

Now I've stopped, I've had time to rethink that reaction. I'm embarrassed. So much so that if I see them again, I am going to tell them so. I thought about writing them letters, but I'm a bloke, so that's a no-no.

When you give up, you'll reminisce about times with your closest friends. You'll think about how nice it would be to have one last evening in the pub, just one more night out. You'll remember the good times you had with them. These memories won't go away. But you know what? They're not supposed to.

There are occasions when I wish I could go out with my best friends and go wild once again. I have three best mates, so it's not like I have a huge entourage, but I do still think about the good times we had together. However, because they're my closest friends, whilst I'm sure they'd like a night or two of the old me, I know they wouldn't suggest it nor, in their hearts, want me to do it.

When you stop drinking or taking drugs, it's only your real friends who come through for you. They're the ones who congratulate you, support you and learn to adapt to the new you. They're the ones you can count on, and who you need to keep in your life.

I used to drink a lot with my brother-in-law. A man whom I adore and have only ever had great times with.

I know there was probably an element of disappointment for him that we would never be able to drink together again. It's true that we never went too crazy – we had fun, wonderful conversations and thoroughly enjoyed ourselves.

However, from day one his reaction was one of support. He listened, understood and got it. We have the memories, and we still enjoy spending time together. We actually do more now than we did back in the drinking days. And you know what? I still fucking love a good lunch! It has become my favourite meal. So, we still holiday together as families and he and I will talk shit over a long lunch. He can enjoy his wine and I enjoy the company, sunshine and eat what the fuck I want. *Bonnes vacances*!

I can say with hand on heart that giving up booze and drugs, whilst not always easy, is the best thing I have ever done in my life. Do I still miss it? On occasion, yes, but those thoughts only last a short time. I think about everything I have achieved since stopping and the thought of going back just doesn't enter my mind.

Does life become boring? No, it does not. Yes, you must find other things to do to fill your time, but I do so much more now than before (such as writing a fucking book!). My family life has improved, I am better off financially, I am excited by the future, I wake up every day feeling fucking great, I've lost weight and, you know what, I feel pretty fucking smug about it all. It's done and I am very proud of that.

Skint

Being a drinker and a drug taker comes at a price. It's a very expensive hobby. I think I could probably have bought the Isle of Wight with the amount of money I spent over the years.

Here's roughly what I reckon the bill came to.

Fifteen years of cocaine use. I'm going to say I spent £60 per week as that should even out my initial relative infrequency to the latter days of three to four grams a week. It was more expensive in the early days, but a gram of coke is now roughly a £40 affair.

That works out at £46,800 … and, if I'm being honest, it could well be more than that.

Now booze, this one's a little trickier. I've drunk since I was sixteen and I have only really had problems in the later years, but it's still worth having a stab at.

Bear in mind that I'd buy alcohol for both my wife and I, although obviously I would consume the vast majority. I reckon in the latter days I was buying ten bottles of wine a week. Perhaps more.

My recycling bins were clinking boxes of shame. In fact, I remember the day they changed the glass collection from small plastic boxes to full size wheelie bins. All my prayers were answered. No more having to put the overflow in the normal bins, plenty of space now. Nothing worse than placing the old plastic box outside your front door with the lid perched on the top in a vague attempt to hide the fact that it was brimming with bottles.

It's a bit like fat people wearing black; you can try to hide it, but it is really only an attempt. Wheelie bin, that's the way forward! Heavy though and not easy when you have to get it out of the back gate, in the wet, pissed up and wearing slippers. The other downside was when the collection lorry turned them out into the rear container. A Niagara Falls of empty bottles smashing to pieces as you mouth to the neighbour, 'Had a bit of a party at the weekend!' We hadn't.

So, let's say I was spending roughly £6 per bottle of wine. That's when I wasn't already pissed in the off licence, suffering from delusions of grandeur and buying the £30 stuff like some sort of connoisseur bell end.

Let's talk about that, the connoisseur bell end. What the fuck was that all about? Pretending you're Gérard Depardieu, sat in your eighteenth-century vineyard, surrounded by fields of lavender, a Citroen 2CV parked up, huddled around a tasting barrel, glass held aloft as though you're about to experience an offering from God.

No, you're at Dave's flat in Hatfield and you've already had five pints. Some twat (probably me) has bought some expensive wine (mainly because the bottle looks nice) and you're all there, noses in glasses, spouting utter piffle.

'Can you smell the cranberry?'

'Yes, it's almost spiced.'

'There's definitely an oakiness to it.'

'I'm getting hints of vanilla.'

No, you're fucking not. You're sniffing wine.

I would say ninety per cent of people have absolutely no clue about wine. And when you get sober you realise that wine smells, well ... like wine. Imagine if it was the same with food. The waiter slops a bit of chicken casserole on your plate and then stands slightly to your side, presenting the dish, waiting for you to have a sniff and signal your approval.

One such event took place at my brother's house. He'd bought a selection of quality wines and decided he'd treat us to a bit of 'blind tasting'. Huddled in the kitchen and with the bottle labels covered over, he poured the first wine delicately into four glasses and handed them round.

We held them aloft against the light like we were trying to look at an eclipse, and twirled our glasses to allow the aromas to flow. On my brother's command, we all took a sip.

Some of us took the next classic connoisseur bell end action of 'slurping'. This creates the type of noise that you'd make when you were five years old and you'd got to the end of your McDonald's milkshake; that really annoying sound which would result in your parents telling giving you a bollocking.

Apparently, the idea is that it draws air over the wine and across your tongue to increase the aroma. In my experience, it does fuck all.

Tasting complete, we all complimented the choice of wine with statements such as 'delicious', 'that's a good one, that' and 'liquid gold'.

It was now results time. All we had to do was answer a simple question: where do you think it's from?

Following a short period of reflection, my brother turned to his wife. The response he was looking for was the Loire Valley.

She sniffed again, took another sip, held the glass aloft and replied, 'Tesco?' Utterly brilliant.

Right, back to the figures. Let's use the fifteen years as a basis and we'll round it down to eight bottles per week.

That's £37,440 worth of booze, not counting drinks out, holidays, 'big nights', etc.

The cost of my nights out were frankly ridiculous. Everyone's rich when they're pissed, right? I simply wouldn't give a shit how much it cost, as long as I had enough booze … and coke. This is also why drinking at home has become so popular. These days, it's so expensive to go out and drink. Pub prices in the UK aren't what they were, especially in fancy London Town. Come to Paris for a beer and you'll need to consider remortgaging your home. I once went for a drink with two mates in a little bar in the Opéra district. We had a couple each, nothing more. The bill was €60. For six pints of

Kronenbourg. The owner muttered something about the cost of rent. We quickly fucked off.

So, I would say that total spent on alcohol can easily be rounded up to £60,000

Let's add the £46,800 spent on cocaine (again, this could be more), which makes the tidy sum of £106,800. That's the price of a house in some areas, spent on getting fucked.

What's mad though is that I regarded these costs as essential items. In a sense, I wouldn't really count it. I'd make flippant comments from time to time about how expensive shopping had become, but it was never the extra 10p on broccoli that was rinsing me of cash.

Rinse me it did though, and once I'd paid the bills, I was spending all the money I earnt and sometimes more (isn't that what credit cards and loans are for?) every month on booze and drugs.

I was one of the lucky ones; I just about managed to keep a grip on my finances. But only just. All my extra money went into my drink and drug habit. If I had £40 left in my account at the end of the month, I know what I'd spend it on.

Thankfully for her, my wife and I always had separate bank accounts. This was useful for me as she didn't get to bear witness to the sheer amount of money I was blowing. Cash withdrawals were the thing. Drug dealers don't yet accept Visa and I never liked being in debt to them, so I always paid my way. But God it cost a lot, and I count myself as one of the fortunate ones who just about held it together financially; many don't.

I knew a guy who eventually went to rehab. He's come out of it a shining example of what rehab can do for some people – he turned it right around and is now happily sober. But he was bad. Really bad. Lost his job, £30K in debt and a complete wreck, but he'd managed to keep it a secret and justify it for years.

That's the thing, you will always justify it. I bought hardly any new clothes, ran the same car for ten years, changed credit cards to move debt around and occasionally used our joint account to see me out of trouble.

The issue is you see it all as essential, especially booze. How many people do I know who are always skint at the end of every month, in debt, living in their overdraft, yet they will happily buy ten bottles of wine a week and spend like Jay-Z when they go out?

The money that comes back to you when you get sober is astounding. I am richer than I have ever been, and I am not earning much more. I even have savings! Fucking spare money! That was never even a thing before, I would spend it all. Oh, the things I could have bought.

I've always wanted a Porsche. I know, what a wanker. But I like cars and Porsches are pretty good. I could easily have owned one, not a new one, but maybe a second-hand Porsche 911. No, instead that went up my nose. And I bought a second-hand Mini.

I know. Wanker.

I will buy a Porsche though, one day. And there'll be only one reason I'll have been able to; because I made a life-changing decision, I got sober. When I turned my life around, everything changed. Opportunities have arisen. In fact, what happened to me is in many ways not dissimilar to Samuel L. Jackson:

'I had a very good theatre reputation. Granted, I was a fucking drug addict and I was out of my mind a lot of the time, but I had a good reputation. Showed up on time, knew my lines, hit my marks. I just wasn't making a lot of money, but I was very satisfied artistically. I was doing Pulitzer prize-winning plays. I was working with people who made me better, who challenged me. So I was doing things the right way, it was just that one thing that was in the way – my addiction. And once that was out of the way, it was – boom! The door blew wide open.'

Boredom

One of the best books I've ever read is Viktor Frankl's *Man's Search for Meaning*. It's part-autobiography about the author's experience in the most notorious Nazi concentration camps and part-psychological analysis on how people value and perceive life. What makes it unique is that it provides a vision of hope and meaning to what must have been one of the most horrendous situations imaginable to woman or man – wondering on a daily basis whether you would live or die. It details how belief, determination and the ability to cling on to hope managed to keep some of those people alive.

I never thought a book written at the end of the Second World war about survival in a Nazi death camp would help me with my drink and drug problems, but it struck a massive chord.

The following passage from the book talks about one of the main issues which addicts like me face. It's one I believe affects every person abusing drugs and alcohol – combatting boredom.

> The existential vacuum manifests itself mainly in a state of boredom. Now we can understand Schopenhauer when he said that mankind was apparently doomed to vacillate eternally between the two extremes of distress and boredom. In actual fact, boredom is now causing more problems to solve than distress. And these problems are growing increasingly crucial, for progressive automation will probably lead to an enormous increase in the leisure hours available to the average worker. The pity of it is that many of these will not know what to do with all their newly acquired free time.
>
> Let us consider, for instance 'Sunday neurosis,' that kind of depression which afflicts people who become aware of the lack of content in their lives when the rush of the busy week is over and the void within themselves becomes manifest. Such widespread phenomena as depression, aggression and addiction are not understandable unless we recognise the existential vacuum underlying them. This is also true of the crises of pensioners and aging people.

Who would believe a book published in 1946 could be so relevant in the twenty-first century?

You see, drugs and drinking are what we do in our spare time. They fill a void.

I will concentrate more on drinking here due to its social acceptance and because of my own experience.

Drinking is something to do. A time filler. For many it's purely a social one, but for us problem drinkers, it's our 'go to' boredom resolver. So much of our time revolves around drinking. Seriously, that's one of the biggest dilemmas you're faced with when you stop – what the fuck am I going to do with all this time on my hands?

You see, Frankl is right; the modern era has created vast amounts of free time. Most people will complain that they're massively busy, that the weekends fly by and the days simply aren't long enough. Funny though, that there's always enough time for a drink.

The reality is that when you're drinking, you're essentially doing fuck all else. Yes, you can argue that you are socialising and I get that, but here we're talking about problem drinkers, home drinkers. Those where the shift has moved away from being social to necessity.

I'm writing this during the Covid pandemic. At the moment I'm in France and under lockdown and in truth, because I can't leave the house, I actually prefer the working week to the weekends.

I'm not a sicko, or a workaholic and I'm not brown-nosing in case my boss reads this book – the reality is that in this current lockdown situation the working week offers me more structure and routine than the weekend. I can only imagine the effect this must be having on those of you who have problems with drink and drugs and have been placed on furlough schemes. Weeks with nothing to do but fuel your addictions, and through no fault of your own. I dread to think what would have happened if I hadn't got sober before this pandemic; it would have been a green light to get fucked every day. I believe it will have devastating effects on the people with addiction problems and even contribute to the creation of new ones.

The difficulty is that the weekend under lockdown has created periods of boredom and whilst I know I will never drink again, the thought has occasionally entered my head. It also brings back the frustration that I mentioned earlier of 'why can't I be a normal drinker', then I could ease the boredom with a drink or two ... or twenty.

I'll talk more about this later, but boredom is the biggest thorn in your side when it comes to sobriety. You must replace the time you spend drinking with other things. If you don't, you'll almost certainly go back to your old habits.

Rock Bottom Moment

You don't necessarily need to have a rock bottom moment, but I know a lot of people do, myself included.

It could be something as simple as a comment from your kids about your favourite thing in the world being wine or it could be a full-on descent into hell where you lose everything you have. Whatever form it takes, it will be the moment you know things simply cannot go on the way they are. A point that makes you realise you can no longer hide from what's going on. It will no doubt be hard and horrible; it will shake your foundation to the core.

It won't be something that makes you realise you *need* to change, it will be something that makes you *want* to change. After all, getting sober isn't for people who need it, it's for people who want it. The need for change will have been realised a long while ago, but until the 'want' comes, you'll happily put it off.

It's at that time you know you cannot go on like this any longer. You know full well that all options have failed. You're

Hitler in the bunker, you're out of solutions and you're fucked.

However, unlike Hitler, you're probably not a mass murderer and whilst we're all glad he's dead; you don't need to be.

There's a way out. And the way out is good.

My rock bottom happened on Friday 10th May 2019.

In many ways it started the day before. I had agreed to go and watch a football match in a bar with a mate on the Thursday night. We started off gently at mine with some drinks and dinner, all very civilised, and then off we went to watch the game.

I have two young kids and, as already mentioned, I tended to do most of my drinking at home. I had actually been off drugs for a few months and was kind of chuffed that coke was out of the picture, so felt I was on track with just being a 'drinker'.

Going out that night felt like a bit of a release – it was a Thursday, nearly the weekend and like most drinkers I'd cleared my work diary for the next day to allow for the fact that I'd no doubt be hungover and completely ineffective at the office.

Out we went and drink we did. Nothing bad happened, in fact it was a great evening. Our football team won, and we even stayed and watched the next game. We met some fun people and the night was a success. However, I drank a lot. I consumed many pints of strong beer, followed by rounds of shots with our new friends. No doubt a lot of bullshit was spoken, talk of, 'we must meet up and do this again!' We did not.

Man Gets Sober

I left the bar pretty drunk. I was all over the place to be honest, but I made it home circa 2 a.m. and crashed out in bed. Ready to be on form for the next day.

I woke up in the morning still pissed. Alcohol still running through me. You know when you get up and pretend you feel fine, but in fact you're still hammered?

As a side note, one thing that scares me now that I'm sober is how many times I got in the car in the morning after a heavy night and drove. We will not even touch the car keys during a night out, but hey, after six pints, copious shots, and four hours sleep, you're fine, right? Shocking.

I got to work and knew I had to get through the day. On the plus side I'd organised a work drinks event for that evening. An invite sent out in the week to all my colleagues, simply titled 'Royal Baby'. Meghan had just given birth and seeing as I'm British, well surely that was a reason to celebrate? I set things up for a 6 p.m. start at the bar over the road from work.

But I was feeling like shit and started wondering how I would get through the day.

The answer was simple, lunch – with more booze.

Lunch would allow me to drink, take the hangover away, get back on it and see me through until the evening. I always had a hit list of colleagues who I knew would be willing participants in a lunch 'out', so I quickly set about contacting them. They took the bait and we arranged to meet at midday. I was fucking delighted.

As always, I was there at twelve on the dot. My colleagues were running late. Perfect, I could have a pint on my own whilst waiting. I ordered a strong Belgian beer and made sure I finished it before they arrived, something which proved to be very easy.

They turned up and I ordered another beer and then another. It was only three pints, but I could feel the effects literally topping me up from the night before.

We finished our meal and then things started to go really wrong. The restaurant owner, who knows us well, offered us a digestif. Candy to a kid for me; I was in. Boom! A massive double brandy to finish the meal off.

With me now somewhat pissed, I engaged full bell-end mode and started chatting to other people in the bar. More drinks were offered, but my colleagues sensibly declined. I did not.

I drank another double brandy, then saw some sense (albeit short-lived) and left the bar.

Back in the office, I was drunk, but fun drunk. It was Friday afternoon, we had drinks planned at 6 p.m., so I thought I'd head out and buy some sweets and snacks as a nice gesture for my colleagues.

I did indeed buy treats for my colleagues, but for some fucking stupid reason, I also bought a quarter bottle of vodka for myself. I think I thought I'd just stay on the buzz for the afternoon, and that would be a good idea.

It was not. In fact, it proved to be a very bad decision.

Over the following two hours, I drank all the vodka. I was now inebriated, and I knew it. I felt as though a huge weight was pushing me to the ground and I didn't know if I wouldn't be able to stand. I knew I was in trouble.

I managed to stagger to the toilets and lock myself into a cubicle.

Then something happened to me that I had never experienced before. I blacked out. I'm not sure how long it was for, but I came to, lying on the floor of the cubicle.

All I could think of was how I could make myself feel better and less drunk. It was almost impossible, and I sat there for another half an hour just trying to pull myself together.

Then my phone rang. It was one of my colleagues.

'Where are you? We're all at the bar – are you coming?'

My immediate thought was what the fuck am I going to do? I didn't want to go, I was in no state to go, but I felt I had no choice. It was, after all, me who had organised the event. Eventually I exited the toilet cubicle and took some deep breaths. I had to get through this, I had to straighten up, I had to go.

I left the office, just about OK, but very conscious that I was drunk. My mind was back and relatively clear, but I wasn't in a good place.

When I got to the bar I think it was obvious I was not sober. In fact, let me change that. It was clear as day that I was fucked.

The proceedings then went like this: I ordered a beer, sat down and managed to drink about half of it before spilling the rest over myself. It looked like I'd pissed myself. Then my boss phoned. I have no idea what we spoke about, but I remember keeping it short as I knew I wasn't making much sense. I was drunk and everyone knew it.

The embarrassment started to flow over me. The shame, the horror.

I knew people must have been wondering why I was already smashed at 6 p.m. I knew I couldn't tell my colleagues the truth, and to this day, I don't know what I said. And I don't want to know.

What did happen was that some of my close colleagues stopped me drinking. They gave me coke (Coca-Cola – not the other sort. Mind you, I would have happily taken it.) This also heightened the acute shame and embarrassment I was feeling. I was in a hole, in a situation where I had publicly highlighted my problem and I knew it.

As can often be the case, this wasn't how my colleagues saw the situation – they told me afterwards that it was funny, but to me it was devastating. I'd lost control at a completely inappropriate time and was deeply ashamed of my actions.

Then phase two came along. The icing on the cake.

My wife phoned.

What she said to me is probably what ended it all. It took me to my lowest point. The moment I knew that a line had been crossed and the game was up.

The conversation was straight forward.

'Where are you?'

'In a bar with colleagues.'

Even after this short exchange she knew I was drunk.

'You did pick up the kids, didn't you?'

With those words, my world stopped. There I was, in a bar, drunk, beer all over my trousers, having recently blacked out at work and I had forgotten to pick up my children.

That was what it took. That was my rock bottom moment.

I did manage to collect them with the help of a colleague, and was only thirty minutes late, but I knew there and then that this was not how I wanted to live my life.

It shocked me to the core. I looked in the mirror and finally saw what I was, what I had become.

There had been many other times when I had been riled with guilt and shame about my drinking, but never so publicly.

That was it, that was what it took for me to make the decision to quit alcohol.

Your rock bottom moment can be anything. Some would argue mine wasn't that bad, and not very rock 'n' roll. There was no police chase, no tigers in a Vegas hotel room, no intervention from my family. But it stopped me in my tracks instantly. I could suddenly see with clarity, and I knew in myself that I *wanted* to change. This desire to change became more important than anything else.

To conclude the story, my wife came to the bar. She felt she had to, if only to check the kids were alright. She stayed for one drink and I started to sober up. By the time we left, I felt the worst of the drunkenness had passed, but inside I was dying.

The next day, I sent out texts of apology. Most responses were kind, but one of my close colleagues asked to talk to me.

I didn't want to speak to him, but I did. He is one of the nicest people I know, and I owed it to him. He said that he'd seen me in the office. Absolutely fucked. Incoherent. I remember none of this. The crazy thing is that he was annoyed with himself. He was annoyed that he didn't get me out of the building and home. Little did he know that by not doing so, he saved me.

He saved me because if I had gone home, I may not have reached rock bottom. I may have got away with it. Learnt a lesson, yes, but avoided the public shame that changed everything.

I am therefore thankful to him, and have since told him so.

Without what happened, I may still be drinking today. Or dead.

What about my wife in all this?

She did the right thing.

She didn't shout or scream. She simply said that I had to stop doing this to myself. Find a way. There were no more chances. I was not the person she knew I could be. She knew the boy she had met twenty years earlier was in there somewhere, but my issues had to be addressed in one form or another.

She pointed out all the good qualities that I had, and the beautiful things there were in my life. She guided me in the right direction. As a person without issues themself, that's all you can do.

This time, I knew she was right and I knew for myself that the time was right. It was now that I needed to stop and, more importantly, there was nothing I desired more.

How to Help People With a Problem

Here's the part of the book you need to share with your partner, family or friends. I would suggest they read the whole thing, but here's where they come in.

I've mentioned time and again that it's you and you alone who can stop drinking or taking drugs. You can get help, yes, but ultimately it comes down to the individual and their desire to stop.

A fleeting effort won't work, moderation won't work, tough love doesn't work. Sadly, as Russell Brand so correctly points out, abstinence is the only way:

'If you have the illness or disease of addiction or alcoholism, the best way to tackle it is not use drugs in any form whether it's state-sponsored opus like methadone or illegal street drugs.'

Abstinence is a scary word, at least for me it was. How on earth could I live my life without ever having a drink again? Drugs I could probably forsake, but I would lose so much by giving up alcohol. That is what I truly believed.

The first time I tried to give up drinking and drugs was a half-baked effort. It was again triggered by me being 'caught out' by my wife. I'd been drinking one Wednesday afternoon when I was supposed to be working. She phoned, and I asked her what time she was picking the kids up from school.

In France, kids don't go to school on Wednesday afternoon.

The guilt rose up inside me, I knew I was in trouble. I went straight home and I confessed that I had a problem. This was the first time I'd admitted it, but in many ways, I only did it to appease the situation.

I hate conflict. I'm no good at it. I realised that if I admitted my troubles and said that I'd stop, there was a good chance the situation would be calmer than if I tried to lie my way around things.

It worked. There were still tears and a difficult conversation, but there was acceptance from my wife.

The problem was on my side. I had just entered into a contract that I wasn't ready to sign.

I didn't really want to stop the drink and drugs, but I now felt I had to. I had no choice – I had to make the effort, do what's right for my wife and kids.

This occurred just before Christmas 2018. I made a plan (more on this later), but I was essentially set up for failure from the word go. I simply wanted this to be a period of good behaviour which would lead to me being able to go back to booze, but this time as a 'responsible' drinker.

I held it together for about a month. The problem was that it wasn't my own choice to stop, but something that was forced upon me, albeit justifiably.

I capitulated in the February. In my mind I'd proved I could stop if I wanted, so if I just drank responsibly from then on, all would be fine. My wife agreed, to an extent. She had seen I'd made an effort and was not in the 'problem drinker/drug taker' mindset, therefore assumed I'd be able to uphold my end of the bargain.

To be brutally honest, I know there was a part of her that wanted me to be able to achieve this. We have always had a lot of fun together, we very rarely fight and have always enjoyed drinking together. I think there was an ounce of hope when I said I wanted to have the odd beer or two again, so she agreed.

However, as you all know, there was no happy ending. I soon went back to my previous levels of drinking and drug taking, and my lowest moment swiftly followed.

The difference the second time I quit was that I was ready. So too was my wife. In fact, this time she got it one hundred percent right. She helped me.

Shouting and screaming at someone who has a problem doesn't work. It can do quite the opposite. It can flick their 'fuck it' switch and make them go out and use again.

'Saying "if you loved me you wouldn't drink" to an alcoholic makes as much sense as saying "if you loved me, you wouldn't cough" to someone who has pneumonia.' Melody Beattie

No, the way to help is simple. You need to provide structure, support and encouragement. Remind them of who they were before their issues; that there are dreams and plans that can be achieved when they get sober.

You need to do this by talking. Help the person work on a plan and accompany them on their journey. You may also need to make concessions such as removing alcohol from the house, not going to pubs and parties, doing other things together that will distract the person from the triggers that certain situations can and will present.

However, this can only be achieved if you, the problem drinker and/or drug taker, want to accept the help. You can say sorry a thousand times, but the best apology is through action. Only changed behaviour is evidence that the apology is genuine.

As the helper, there may be things in the past that have been deeply upsetting to you. Problem drinkers and drug addicts are selfish mother fuckers and will have no doubt caused you great pain. These things may need to be discussed, but not whilst they are in this initial phase.

Once a person is sober, and stably so, you can look to address the issues that you have as a couple, family or partnership. Dredging up the past can easily cause them to regress. The way ahead needs to be happy and forward looking, not full of nagging and recriminations. The future is where the happiness is, this is the key.

I will say this again though – the decision to quit must be made by the person who has the problem. They have to want to stop. If they don't, they won't, and you have every right to be angry. If you've run out of ultimatums, then maybe it's time to abandon the help. Maybe this will prompt their rock bottom moment. If it doesn't, then you will still have done all you can.

I remember my wife and I going out to dinner about two months after I'd stopped. She told me she was proud of me, that I'd 'come back' and that she was, for the first time in a long time, excited for the future. She focused on the positives, reminded me of the dreams I used to have, my desire to write something, my passion for cars, my love of running, my kindness, my happy soul and all of the things she fell in love with.

She also adapted. I'd stopped drinking and she respected that by not forcing me to do anything that may involve situations that I didn't want to be in. If I didn't want to go to a party, no problem, we wouldn't go. She had a 'whatever it takes' attitude. I cannot tell you how much I respect her for that.

You see, you will go through change. The biggest change of your life. Your life will be better – I guarantee you that – but also very different. Your partner, friends and family need to understand, accept and embrace this. Especially at the beginning.

In my opinion there are a number of the things they should concentrate on.

Physically giving up drinking or taking drugs is not difficult. You simply stop the act of putting it in your body. Mentally though, it's something else altogether. The FOMO will strike (regularly) and you will be susceptible to the 'fuck it' moments'.

As a partner, friend or family member, you need to constantly remind people who have taken this big decision just how good they have become. Remind them how brave they are. They have stopped doing something that so many other people have problems with.

Tell them they have a superpower so many others don't have. They have the power not to drink or take drugs. That makes them unique. Genuinely, there aren't many people in the world who can do this.

Talk about the differences it has made to them and to your lives. Remind them every day just how nice it is to be with them.

Treat them like you would someone who's been in hospital, spoil them, get them tickets to a football game, take them to a concert, even if you don't even want to. Do things with them you've never done before. Go to places you've never been.

Look at this as a new adventure. You'll soon see that without drugs and alcohol, so much more can be achieved together.

Be proud of them.Tell them how proud you are, and tell others too. Take pride in the fact that your partner doesn't drink or use; be proud that your best mate had the fucking balls to stand up, acknowledge their problem and sort themselves out.

Tell them that they look better. Talk to them about their dreams. Suggest they do things with the money they are saving. In short, embrace their new life and yours.

On the other hand, there are also things you need to avoid.

Shouting and screaming. This solves nothing. Also, they may slip up; it happens. You cannot expect someone to get over something they've been doing for years in one go.

Like anything new, it takes practice. Some people might keep the it up from day one. Others, like me the first-time round, might skip practice for a while. However, they can come back to it and many people do.

Try and put your problems on hold. Concentrate on one thing at a time. You know for a fact that a sober person will make better, clearer and more concise decisions. Give them the time they need and then work on any big decisions that need to be made.

If you yourself drink, fine, but talk to the person about it. See how they feel. Some people want all alcohol removed from the house. This wasn't the case for me, but if it is for them, try to respect this and come to an agreement.

If you take away only one thing, let it be this. Every day is a new day. If they slip up, they can start again tomorrow. As a partner, friend or family member, it will not be your fault.

It's so very complex, the mind of a problem drinker or drug user. Errors can happen. Don't immediately sit and think, 'Fucking hell, here we go again.' Talk to them. Tell them it's OK, that you're still proud of what they've achieved and that very few people get to where they're going the first time, but when they do, they become superheroes.

Here's a little story about superheroes. A true one.

When I was a kid, I had a best friend who, for confidentiality reasons, I am going to call Luke. He and I lived opposite each other, he was a couple of years older than me, but we were inseparable.

We met when I was about ten and remained very close until I was sixteen. We did everything together, from mountain biking to shooting air rifles to chasing girls and drinking when we hit our adolescent years. We even holidayed together numerous times.

On one occasion we went to the Isle of Wight with my parents. I know it was towards the latter years of our friendship because Luke could drive, and my Mum had kindly let him use her red 1990 Volvo 240 estate. Look it up, it's basically a tank.

One day we loaded our bikes into the back of the car and headed out to a forest to tear around for a few hours. After an hour or so biking, we headed up a large hill and sat down to take a breather. We had brought drinks and snacks and broke them out to replenish our energy.

It was on this hill, looking out over the woods and the stunning fields of the Isle of Wight that a suddenly emotional Luke told me that he had a secret. Something he'd been hiding for quite some time but wanted to share with me.

He told me he was suffering from bulimia.

Being a fifteen-year-old boy, my initial reaction was, 'What the fuck is bulimia?' I wondered if I might catch it, and whether I'd need cream?

For those of you who don't know, bulimia is an eating disorder and mental health condition.

According to the NHS website, anyone can get bulimia, but it is more common in young people aged 13 to 17. Sufferers binge eat and then make themselves sick to stop gaining weight. It can lead to dramatic weight loss, severe health problems and even death.

Having learnt more about this illness as I got older, I see many similarities to problem drinkers or drug takers. Whilst the issue involves a physical action, namely sticking your fingers down your throat, it's the mental part that must be overcome.

Luke explained that he would eat and make himself sick. He couldn't stop, even though he knew it was wrong. He had done it twice that morning and had been doing it every day of our holiday.

I look back at this day and think how fucking brave he was to tell me this. Though, as you will find out at the end of this little story, it is no surprise that he found that bravery within himself.

I tried to support Luke as best I could. I'm not sure if I did a good job of it or not.

Luke had a dream. He wanted to join the army. More than that, he wanted to be an officer in the Parachute Regiment. To achieve this goal, he knew he had to be at the peak of his mental and physical fitness and of course, that would mean that he had to find a way to overcome his bulimia.

Clearly the help and support he received from doctors played a part in his recovery, but there was one event that I remember being a turning point.

To train for his impending entrance selection to Sandhurst Military Academy, Luke would run every day, often with bricks in a rucksack to improve his stamina. On one occasion, he set off and had got a mere 100 metres down the road when he came across a group of children in wheelchairs being pushed by their carers. As he ran past with his rucksack of bricks and his trademark smile, one of the kids managed to turn his head and utter a word to Luke.

'Superman'.

One word.

That word changed everything.

This simple exchange clarified everything for Luke. It upset him terribly, because that one word spoken from a person whose life really was a challenge made him realise what he actually had in his own life. He was a young, fit, dynamic individual who's only remaining barrier was bulimia.

I believe this was the biggest and most authentic compliment Luke had ever received. The fact that it came from a stranger made it incredibly poignant. It wasn't from a friend or family member trying to pander to the situation they knew he was in. It was completely genuine.

Soon afterwards the posters went up. He taped the word 'Superman' above each toilet in his house. A poignant reminder to help when the physical part of his illness was trying to break through. What's more, it was there for everyone to see. He'd had his rock bottom moment and he was now on the way up.

That one comment helped Luke get better and, more importantly, it helped change the image he'd always had of himself. When Luke was younger, he was overweight and hated it, and that is how he had continued to view himself.

That boy that I still know became a very high-ranking officer in the British Army.

In 2008 he led 200 soldiers from the British Army's legendary Parachute Regiment on a six-month tour of the most dangerous part of Afghanistan.

At the end of the deadly tour, that boy who sat on a hill and told me he had bulimia was awarded the British Military Cross for 'leadership and gallantry under fire'.

Health, But Who Gives a Shit?

I'm not going to dwell on the medical side of drinking or drug taking.

You can easily find a huge amount of information about the damage alcohol and drugs do to your health. As previously stated, I'm not a doctor and so it's not for me to go into detail on the health risks of these two activities.

Having said that, I will share with you what I have noticed personally. This will be quick, much like my toilet habits when I was drinking and taking drugs.

I had the shits. A lot. And my shit stank.

Please don't dwell on that for too long.

My grandmother died some time ago now, having reached the ripe old age of ninety. She could also fart and destroy a toilet better than anyone I've ever known. Bless her.

Whether it was getting in the car, at the dinner table or simply standing up, she'd pass wind. I don't mean a silent squeak or a one off 'Oh I'm sorry' type of fart, no. It would go on for several seconds. 'Parp, parp, parp, parp, paaaaaarr.'

There was no hiding it and she was better at farting than me or any of my friends (and trust me, I can fart!). Night on the beer, curry, kebab, Jägermeister shots … nothing could generate wind better than my grandma. When it occurred in public, it was like the fireworks at a Disney parade. People would stop and look in awe, wide-eyed, open-mouthed. I swear on the odd occasion there was even light applause.

However, if truth be told, she was terribly embarrassed by it. As her loving family, we said nothing. We got used to it and didn't even react when Grandma launched into a twenty-minute fart-a-thon. The fact was her bowels were a nightmare for many years.

The reason I'm telling you this is that when I drank and took drugs, I too had terrible bowels. Liquid poo was a very common occurrence, as were stomach aches.

I put it all down to my grandma and genetics. I simply believed, or wanted to believe, that this was all occurring due to some sort of hereditary issue. Sadly, I didn't reach the heady heights of my fart-machine Gran, but to me, this was why I wasn't shitting normally. I was a Kerrison, so I must have inherited the gene. If there even is a shitting gene.

When I stopped drinking and taking drugs, my toilet troubles immediately ceased. My grandmother was tee total, so for her it was a genuine problem, but for me this was not the case.

Now, I'm a healthy 'poo in the morning' type of guy. No more upset stomachs, no more pebble dashing, just a nice relaxing crap before work.

I'll let you enjoy that image.

I also suffered from heartburn.

Here's the thing, if you've never had heartburn before and then you suddenly get it, you basically think you are going to die. Seriously.

Sunday nights were the killer for me. Usually after a weekend bender. It would strike once I'd got into bed.

Heartburn, bad heartburn, makes you feel like you're having a heart attack.

It would always last about an hour, no matter how many antacid tablets I took or how much milk I drank (milk helps), it would hit me like a train and, on some occasions, genuinely scare me.

I remember once, my wife was away and I was in bed with heartburn, or what I hoped was heartburn. It was so bad, I started to believe that it really could be a heart attack.

I was alone with the kids. What if I died?

I actually feared for my life. I was petrified.

It did eventually go away and, of course, wasn't enough to cease my habits. But since stopping alcohol and drugs, I've not had heartburn again. Not once.

In terms of the other damage drink and drugs can do, we all know about these little beauties:

Heart disease.

High blood pressure.

Stroke.

Liver disease.

Cancer of the breast, mouth, throat, esophagus, liver, colon.

Jaundice.

Death (caused by any of the above).

But who gives a shit, right?

Honestly, until it's too late, I would argue that very few people give two fucks about the potential health issues that can be caused by drugs and alcohol.

I didn't.

You see, we all think we're invincible, and in many ways it's a fortunate thing that we do. I'm quite sure if the human race didn't have this trait then no fucker would have gone up Everest, shot themselves out of a canon or tried to imitate Bishop from *Aliens* with a knife.

But the fact remains we're incredibly good at convincing ourselves we're immortal and things won't happen to us.

One example is my huge consumption of red wine. I managed to twin the idea that because someone once said that red wine could have potential health benefits, and that I mainly drank red wine, I would never succumb to any health problems.

This, I now know, is utter bollocks.

But the problem drinker or drug taker will tell themselves anything to make it OK, and as is often the case, so will your entourage. Egging you on to have another, even accusing you of being a women's vagina for not wanting a drink.

It's utterly farcical when you think about it. You're literally pushed to take something that may kill you. This is particularly true with booze – alcohol is the only drug I know that you have to apologise for not taking.

It's only when it is too late that our friend Mr Hindsight comes knocking on the door. When you're fucked and the problems are incurable.

It's mad. But it won't stop people. It certainly didn't stop me.

My personal opinion is that doctors could do more. The message isn't strong enough. I know people who are overweight, drink too much and have high blood pressure as a result. The answer? Once the person has no doubt lied about the number of units of alcohol they consume each week, they'll be given some blood pressure pills and sent home to carry on.

No plan, no scary message, no moral story – not like smoking.

'Here are some pills for your dangerously high blood pressure. Drink?'

As I've already said, I do understand this. I get it, so it's very difficult for me to even try and change this perception. But if you recognise yourself in this, then, well, you know and on your head be it if it gets you in the end.

The Mental Problem

I may be slated for this. It's controversial I know, but this is just a normal guy writing a book about his own experiences, views and thoughts on how to quit drinking and drug taking. It's not a medical journal. It's not a piece for the BBC. It's one man's ideas and advice based on his own situation and ways of dealing with addiction.

I do not believe that the majority of people who have issues with alcohol or drugs have a disease. A mental health problem, yes, but not a disease. There, I said it.

To me, it doesn't fit the definition of a disease. You don't contract it, it is not caused by infection, it is not contagious and it does not come in the form of outbreaks.

Let me give you my simple reasoning and forgive me if you find it offensive.

If you have a drink or drug problem and I lock you in a room without alcohol or drugs, you will get better. Yes, it would be horrific, but if you had no other underlying illnesses, you would recover. Physically anyway – some people would say that in extreme cases people may die, but the majority would not.

If you have cancer and I did the same experiment, you would die. Without medical intervention there is nothing you can do personally that can stop the spread. There is no 'choice'. The disease would take hold and kill you.

However, disease or no disease, to me, the biggest health issue that affects all problem drinkers and drug takers is the one we talk about the least. The one we talk about the least in life, full stop. What is going on in our head.

You see, the mind is a fucking cunt!

For me, it's the mind, not the body, that locks people into destructive behaviour. Everybody's mind talks to them, some more than others, and I even physically talk to myself. 'First sign of madness!' my mother would say, as she too would happily gabble away on her own when she thought no one was around.

The beauty of the mind, though, is also its greatest downfall. Everything it tells you is a secret!

No one, not even the best scientists or doctors in the land can get into your head and read your thoughts. No, your thoughts are for you and you alone, unless you choose to share them.

The beauty, then, is that the mind can think, plan, create, imagine and reflect. It can reassure you, allow you to make decisions, dream and fantasise. All of which can be done in the utmost secrecy.

The mind can also fool you. It can do this in many ways, and some are indeed medical conditions. But for us regular problem drinkers and drug users, the one that we fall foul of time and again is the mind's ability to reassure us.

It reassures us that maybe we don't have an issue. Maybe someone else has bigger troubles than us. It tells us that it doesn't matter, that our problem isn't really affecting us. It tells us that one day we'll stop, and it does the most amazing job of rationalising all of this and making everything all right, even when we know it isn't.

In our secret heads, we still try and convince ourselves that all is fine and fucking dandy.

And the worst thing about it all is we keep it to ourselves. Under no circumstances must anyone know.

The thing is, everyone has a natural self-preservation button in their head. It's human nature. Therefore, we lie. Some more than others, but we *all* lie. Even my kids and they are annoyingly good at it.

I once spent two hours on a beach looking for my son's glasses.

'I am sure I put them down on my towel before I went in the sea, Daddy' he said.

We were a group of ten friends on the beach that day – we all searched. Under towels, under other people's towels; buckets, bags, even bins were emptied. Nothing.

Eventually we gave up and assumed that they must have got accidently buried under the sand and we'd simply have to get him a new pair. So be it. Shit happens.

A few days later I heard my son and his cousin chatting in the kitchen and something caught my attention – the word 'glasses'.

I quickly moved in, serious look on my face, ready to do some proper parenting.

After some stern, yet fair discussion and the obligatory, 'I promise I won't be angry, just a long as you tell the truth,' the real version of the story came out.

In the boys' rush to get into the sea, my son had forgotten to take his glasses off. They'd bombed down the beach straight into the surf and boom, my son took a wave head on, and his glasses were gone. Despite waving his hands around under the water like swans' feet in a vague attempt to find them, they were no more.

Both boys knew the truth and had decided not to tell. Accomplices I believe they are called.

Two. Fucking. Hours.

Digging, searching, sand in every orifice, only to find out that the little shits had lied all along! The thing is, once they'd told me, it made everything alright. I actually found it quite funny, and part of me was even impressed that they'd managed to keep tight lipped for so long. But they'd lied, kept the truth in their heads. This time it didn't really matter, but it's this ability, the fact that we can internalise everything and lie, that can so often descend us into mental hell.

We *all* have our issues, yet we find it so difficult to talk about them. Especially men. We just don't do it.

The reality is that we could all tell the truth about what's happening in our lives, what it's doing to us and in some cases, but not all, why. But we don't.

Because we can't get inside people's heads, we often look for other ways to help, such as more drugs, albeit legal ones. In some cases, this works, but for many it doesn't, and that person will forever wrestle with their demons without saying a word to anyone.

This is the addict's Achilles heel. We don't want to tell anyone what's really going on in our mind. We don't want people to know that we have a problem. We don't want them to know that maybe we are down there with the dregs of society, because isn't that the image of an addict?

What I found, though, is that the worse the problem gets, the more we lie, the more we descend into self-loathing. Much of this is justified, after all alcohol and drugs affect the mind. We've all done stupid and bad things when under the influence. Things we regret, things we wish we could change, things we tell ourselves that we will never do again, but back we go, time and time again.

The way we feel about ourselves and what goes on in our heads are the hardest things to change. We can get ourselves into real trouble with our thoughts and feelings.

So, what's the answer to this? In many cases people resort to alcohol and drugs to suppress the things in their head. Suppress them it may, but it does not make them go away.

I once heard that you shouldn't ask an addict, 'Why do you do what you do?', but 'What happened to you?'

Bad things do happen to some people. Very bad things. I cannot even begin to imagine what it must be like to have been abused, neglected, raped. I can only imagine these experiences can drive people to drink and drugs as a way to numb the pain and forget.

However, it never gets rid of the fact that these things happened. Only by talking and seeking the right help can the issues that drive behaviour be addressed. You must seek the help that is available.

What I also want to say is you don't have to have had a bad life or experience to become addicted to drugs and alcohol and, dare I say it, we sometimes look for excuses to fuel our drink and drug habits.

I see a lot of Instagram posts and the like talking about how addiction can always be linked to trauma, often when young. I get this, I really do, and I can see that in many cases this is true, but not all. I am one of those examples. Nothing especially dreadful happened to me, but I still ended up being an addict.

What also needs to be considered is that some people may have gone through equally bad times and horrific experiences, but do not go down the route of drink and drug addiction. Drink and drugs may be your coping mechanism, but the point is there are people out there who have the same grief, the same troubles and do manage to deal with these things without turning to substance abuse.

What I am trying to say, is that there is a life after addiction. People do get over trauma, or at least learn to manage it, not easily, but they find a way, seek the right help. That person can be you.

Also, you and I know damn well that dealing with those 'root' issues when sober is going to give you a far better chance of getting over them than continuing with the bottle or a rolled-up bank note. Underlying problems will not go away, but I guarantee that contrary to what you may believe, they will be easier to deal with when you're sober.

One thing I do have experience of are the 'fuck it' moments. Simple rows with your wife, bad days at work, or even just occasions when you're feeling sorry for yourself can provoke a 'fuck it' moment. These are the times when you know damn well you shouldn't be getting drunk or taking drugs, but you do. You're pissed off or upset about something, so you simply go 'fuck it', buy some booze or drugs and partake in the behaviour that you know isn't right, but you do it anyway. Fuck it.

This can then escalate, especially if you're challenged by a family member or partner. I can remember times when my wife would say, 'You're not going to drink much tonight, are you?' That would hit my 'fuck it' button and I would find every conceivable way to drink more. Fuck it, fuck them, fuck you all; I'm an adult and I can do what I want. Yes, that sort of stupid shit.

I do believe though that everyone has something that kicks it all off. For me, I think the party that started when I was young never stopped, and nor did I want it to. I loved the freedom of my youth and I just couldn't adapt to adulthood. I'm not saying this was a reason, but it certainly played a part in both my mental addiction and in turn, my sobriety.

Only talking can get things out in the open. Only dialogue can create a path to resolving your problems. If people don't know what's wrong, they can't help you. There is no other way.

Get the truth out. Trust me, it's liberating. No matter what you've done.

If you can take control of your thinking, your mind and attitude to drink or drugs, then everything else will fall into place. By removing these from your life, it will remove you from the spiral of descent.

The majority of the issues people face *do* have a solution – I like the phrase that there are no problems, only solutions.

However, there is only one way to do this. It takes balls. It will make you squirm. You will feel uncomfortable, but you must do it.

You must talk. You must stop lying. You must be honest with yourself. You must be honest with other people.

If you can do this, if you can pluck up the courage to stop keeping everything in your head, mind-fucking yourself at every corner, if you can just get it out, then you can start getting better.

It's so simple, yet so bloody hard. Just to sit down and say to someone, 'I'm fucked, here's why I'm fucked, and I'd like some help with it please.' It's difficult, but the weight off your shoulders when you do speak these words is incredible. I know, I had that moment, I was in pieces, crying my eyes out. The reality was that the tears were tears of relief. Finally, I had told the truth. I had a problem and I wanted to address it.

It's not easy and sometimes it's only when the lies, destructive behaviour and deceit become more difficult to hide than the truth that people hit rock bottom.

For men, I think it's even tougher.

To openly admit you have a problem is just such a difficult task. Most men don't talk about their problems. I didn't and it made my life so much more complicated than it needed to be.

We don't share what's in our heads. We keep everything to ourselves and pour fuel on the fire by continuing to do the one thing that means we avoid telling the truth or talking – getting fucked.

Trust me once you embrace being honest, it will be liberating, life changing even.

When you're sober, you simply don't fuck up like you do when you're on alcohol or drugs. You don't make the mistakes. Life becomes much simpler. You'll see the wood for the trees. No more apologising, no more hiding things. No more preoccupying your head with what you're going to do about the next situation. No more wondering how you're going to lie your way out of things. No more waking up in the morning with the thoughts of dread about the night before.

All that goes away.

The funny thing is that once you do start clearing your head, you want to do so much more. There is no fucking way on God's earth that I could have even attempted to write a book when I was on the booze and drugs. I could talk about it, oh yes, I was good at that, but putting it into action, actually doing something that I'd talked to someone about, probably pissed in a bar – that never happened.

Now it does.

You too can get to this point.

In my opinion, stopping drinking and taking drugs is ALL in the mind. It's about getting your head around a new life and then talking about it.

Once that happens, it's a very beautiful thing.

Work

Before I got sober, when I look back at my career, I hang my head in shame.

Not due to lack of achievement – I have always worked and had fairly good jobs. Nothing super incredible in terms of seniority, remuneration or status, but I have been fortunate – I have never really hated work (well, apart from when I was in IT recruitment, man that was shit).

I have always followed my father's advice. It was pretty straightforward; he simply told me when I was about sixteen and had no idea what I wanted to do with my life, that it didn't matter what I did, just as long as I went to work.

And work I have. Always. Without fail. I have always had a job.

Even when I was made redundant in 2009, I had a new job within two weeks. I made getting a new job my job. I bought a desk, installed it in the spare bedroom and worked from nine to five contacting friends and former colleagues, searching the Internet and the like. It paid off. Hard work always does.

The shame I feel is because until I got sober, in every job I have had there has been time lost. Not physically, I was never one to pull a sick day because of a massive session on a school night, but there were many times when I would turn up to work hungover as fuck.

On occasions I would even be worried about the stench of booze on me ... after I had driven to the office. It still makes me shudder, that.

There was one company I worked for where I would even spend most of my Fridays in the toilets snorting coke.

I got away with it all. It's in the past and I'm fairly sure that until that fateful afternoon when everything changed, no one noticed. Or so I'd like to think.

But let's be brutally honest, your productivity when hungover at work is fucking awful. Arriving in the morning, praying for the day to end. Please God nothing important come up! Hours spent dicking about on the Internet. I've watched more YouTube videos hungover at work than most people do in a lifetime. Researching holidays, I became good at that. Facebook could while away a few hours, as could chatting shit to people all day.

Hours lost and, more importantly, opportunities lost.

I did have one amazing talent though, one that I see with almost all the office heavy drinkers. The ability to moan about work, constantly. I would happily bang on about how shit the management was, yet be prepared to do absolutely nothing about it. All I would look forward to was the end of the day, so I could go home and have a drink. Reset for the next day.

Do the bare minimum, get paid, moan about the hand I'd been dealt, do fuck all to change it. But when you're a beer boy, you're the bollocks, ain't ya!

Now I've stopped, I realise that this behaviour makes you an utter bell end, and a useless one at that.

Don't get me wrong, I never went into work not wanting to do a good job and I had many successes, but now I am so much more on the ball and it shows. I experience none of the anxiety I used to feel at work. I know what I'm capable of and use those capabilities every day. I use my time better, go out of my way to improve myself and make relationships that count (not the ones with whom I can light a sambuca and stick it to my belly button).

There will be many of you reading this who will know damn well that their drinking is holding them back at work. You know you're basically just sat back doing the bare minimum because when 6 p.m. comes around you can go and do what you're really good at; getting fucked.

It never really mattered what day of the week it was. Monday night? Not a problem, I could easily get absolutely hammered. I would even anticipate it, clearing my diary for the following day or adding some fake meetings to make sure I could do as little as possible after a large weekday session.

There were even times when I took drugs during the week and didn't sleep. Tossing and turning from Tuesday into Wednesday. Lying in bed, coke running through my system, praying for kip. It wouldn't happen and I would just get up. Shattered, but pretending I'd had a great night's rest, and go to work wrecked. Staying awake for two days and going to work, I wasn't effective, I was a zombie with a massive appetite for coffee.

I kept this going for years.

Now I'm not saying that all your work troubles go away when you get sober, but what I can tell you is that it does allow you to give the best representation of yourself when you are working.

Everyone has good and bad days and if, once you've removed booze and/or drugs from your life, work is *still* shit, then you know you need to make a change there too.

My experience has been that since I got sober, every decision I make is one with a clear conscience. If it's wrong, I can quickly identify why. That happened far less often when I was hungover or high. My productivity has skyrocketed. I am fully present, available and simply better at what I do.

This has been evident in my progress – I've received praise, pay rises and serious promotions. My circle of influence has also grown hugely now that I have made a conscious clear-headed effort to make it so.

The final thing, believe it or not, is now that I'm sober, I sleep like a king every night, my diary is full, and I love Mondays.

Recovery

Recovery, a bit like disease, I have trouble with.

I have no experience of rehab centres and the great work they no doubt do, but I hear the word 'recovery' used incredibly often in the context of rehab experiences.

Personally, as a problem drinker and drug taker, an addict, I do not consider myself to be in recovery per se. But then again, I do not consider addiction to be an illness that one recovers from. My belief is that one learns to live with addiction, not recover from it.

Recovery suggests that the person will one day be completely cured. How long does one need to recover? Are you always in recovery? What does recovery mean exactly?

In many ways I think it provides false hope. I don't believe you ever recover; you just stop doing. You live differently to the way you did before.

In fact, I think that anybody who has a problem with alcohol and/or drugs and turns their life around will always have times when they need to think about their sobriety. No matter how long it's been, no matter how old you are, I believe you are only ever one drink, line or hit away from going back.

Recovery gives false hope. It suggests that in time, your issues will go away. Time is the greatest healer, no doubt about that, but at what point is one 'recovered'? Six months, two years, twenty years? There are some people who stop for half a lifetime and then go back. I believe you need to learn to live with the possibility of temptation in the long term and you need to constantly educate yourself as you go along. It's a journey of change. Do you recover? Maybe, but maybe not – if you've had a problem with something and you go back to that something, it will be a problem again. You must learn not to go back to it, not necessarily to recover from it.

I wonder if this old-style terminology is still useful in the modern world. You recover from a cold, a broken leg, but in my opinion you don't recover from addiction. You decide that you don't want to live like that anymore and find another way. You learn to live with it.

When asked if he misses drinking alcohol, he says, 'I mean, we have a winery. I enjoy wine very, very much, but I just ran it to the ground. I had to step away for a minute. And truthfully, I could drink a Russian under the table with his own vodka. I was a professional. I was good.' He adds, 'Don't want to live that way anymore.' Brad Pitt talking to GQ Style

Having said this, I would never criticise anyone who wants to adhere to the concept of being in recovery when they have used it to conquer their demons.

Russell Brand's work on this subject is excellent. Whilst he still refers to disease and recovery, which I totally respect, he has modernised the approach of Alcoholics Anonymous (AA) and their twelve-step programme. His new take on this opens with the most beautiful gambit.

'Are you a bit fucked?'

Followed by, 'Could you not be fucked?'

This is genius and it helps reach more people, especially those who, like me, are not religious. We need this, much more of this, as it brings a more genuine approach to the idea that you can stop if you really want to. New language around sobriety is out there for all to find, but we must make it more mainstream.

Getting sober is about making a choice and providing yourself with enough weapons in your armory to make sure you never forget why you originally made this choice.

You may need to change your weapons as you go along, and possibly rely on them less and less, but keep them close. You never know when you'll need them.

More on those later.

Addiction isn't a Choice

Nobody sets out to get addicted. Nobody.

However, when I hear people say that 'addiction isn't a choice' I have to disagree. We must get away from this ridiculous idea that taking drugs or drinking is somehow forced upon you. It isn't.

I was born in 1975 and throughout the eighties there was a popular drugs campaign that ran for quite a few years with the motto 'Just Say No'. It started in the United States, championed by the First Lady Nancy Reagan during her husband's presidency.

Its purpose was to encourage young people to abstain from illegal substances. In the UK it even gained fame via the cast of a teen TV soap, *Grange Hill*, when they released a song titled *Just Say No*. The single reached number five in the charts and remained in the Top 100 for five weeks. Its purpose was to deliver a clear anti-drug use message, telling listeners to 'just say no' to drugs.

These campaigns had virtually no effect on addiction. For instance, Scientific American found that "JustSay No"-related programs like D.A.R.E did "little or nothing to combat substance use in youth".

Interestingly, I never saw any adverts 'saying no' to alcohol; just ones to encourage use. Nothing's changed there then.

I believe there are massive misconceptions from non-drug users about how people start taking drugs. The infamous image of the 'drug pusher' at the school gates springs to mind. I have done a lot of drugs and throughout my education I never saw a single drug dealer at the school gates (which at the time, I felt was a great shame!)

I have never had drugs pushed onto me. I have been in situations where drugs are available, many times, and I often said 'yes', but this is because I wanted to, not because someone forced me to.

You see most people start out on their drink and/or drug journey because they want to. They see others doing it and want to experience it for themselves. It's great fun at the beginning and for many, they can control their intake. Millions of people have taken all sorts of drugs and walked away from the experience with no issues at all.

The ones like me that don't are different. We seek it out, we want it. Yes, this drives addiction, in fact this is addiction, but at no point was it not my choice. I chose to drink the amounts of alcohol that I did, and I chose to take the cocaine, but at every step of the way, it remained purely my choice.

But in the same way that I chose to get fucked, I also chose to get un-fucked.

It takes work, just as hiding my habit did. But I guarantee that if you invest as much time in getting un-fucked as you did in getting fucked, you'll be amazed at what you can achieve.

Addiction is a choice and one I was happy with for many years. I didn't necessarily look at it as addiction, but I was the one that carried on. I was the one who would buy coke to snort, and I was the one who would open a bottle of wine knowing damn well I would drink the whole thing myself.

I had a choice. Addiction occurred because of those choices and because the substances I was taking were highly addictive.

I then made another choice. The one to stop.

I made that choice. Somewhat under pressure, yes, but the choice came from me and me alone, as it only can for anyone in the same situation.

Addiction is what happens when you choose a life where drink and/or drugs are your life choice.

Choose wisely, I say.

Loser

Here is a list of names:
- Carrie Fisher
- Daniel Radcliffe
- Buzz Aldrin
- Anthony Hopkins
- Stephen King
- Robin Williams
- Jamie Lee Curtis
- Matthew Kerrison
- Kelly Osbourne
- Robert Downey Jr.
- Bradley Cooper
- Ben Affleck
- Ewan McGregor
- Brad Pitt

Elvis Presley

Do you associate this list of names with a bunch of losers, lowlifes, the dregs of society? Probably not.

On this list you have an astronaut. A man who is the recipient of an Academy Award, three BAFTAs, two Emmys, the Cecil B. DeMille Award and who in 1993 was knighted for services to the arts. You have Harry Potter, Princess Leia and Obi fucking Wan Kenobi.

I mean, holy shit! how much fun must it have been on the set of the *Star Wars* films? Swinging a lightsaber about, completely off your tits.

The fact is, none of these people are losers. They have all achieved huge fame, are all household names and are no doubt very rich. Well, all except one. Me.

So why did I add my name to the list?

The first reason is to give some context to the statement that you are a loser if you have drink or drug problems.

You see, being a normal person, if I tell someone I don't know that I have a problem with drugs and alcohol or come straight out and say that I'm an addict, chances are they'll think I'm a useless piece of shit who ended up sleeping on a park bench covered in wee, that I neglected my children, robbed my nan for booze and sold the family home to buy coke.

However, I imagine that if Brad Pitt told someone that he had drink and drug problems, they would simply put it down to his Hollywood lifestyle and still want to touch his bottom.

Here's the list again:

> Carrie Fisher (alcohol, cocaine, MDMA, opioids – narcotic analgesic that is at least part synthetic, not found in nature)
>
> Daniel Radcliffe (alcohol)
>
> Buzz Aldrin (alcohol)
>
> Anthony Hopkins (alcohol)
>
> Stephen King (alcohol and cocaine)
>
> Robin Williams (alcohol and cocaine)
>
> Jamie Lee Curtis (alcohol and opiates – narcotic analgesic derived from an opium poppy)
>
> Matthew Kerrison (alcohol and cocaine)
>
> Kelly Osbourne (alcohol and opioids)
>
> Robert Downey Jr. (alcohol, cocaine ... and pretty much everything)
>
> Bradley Cooper (alcohol and opioids)
>
> Ben Affleck (alcohol)
>
> Ewan McGregor (alcohol)
>
> Brad Pitt (alcohol and marijuana)
>
> Elvis Presley (barbiturates and opiates)

The second reason that I've put my name on the list is to show you I'm the same as all these celebrities. And you are too.

Addiction doesn't give a fuck about fame, money, race, religion or gender. We are all the same. Sure, for those who have more money, they may not experience the financial collapse that drink and drugs can bring, but trust me, they are going through exactly the same emotions, struggles, sadness and hell on earth as regular me and you.

You are not a loser if you are a drink or drug addict. You made bad choices and got hooked on an addictive substance. However, you are a loser if you don't do anything about it.

Most of the people on my list did do something about it. The ones that didn't make it, did at some stage in their lives at least try and overcome their problems.

The world in general must get over the stigmatism of drug and alcohol addiction.

Sadly, I doubt this will happen anytime soon, so it is down to you to get over your own view of yourself in terms of your drink and/or drug problems.

There is always a way out. You found a way in – you can find a way out.

It doesn't matter that you'll have to tell people you have an addiction problem. Fuck them. If you're doing something about it, that's all that matters.

It takes big fucking balls when you're in a situation where your poison of choice is offered to you, and you decline. In fact, it's empowering.

I will admit it's not always easy to come up with your story, your pitch, your elevator speech about why you gave up. I'll share mine later, along with some tips on what to say, depending on the situation you're in or in some cases, how much of an arsehole the person is being who is asking you.

What I will say now is that if they then judge you on this, once they are out of earshot, or their back is turned, extend your middle finger and whisper, 'Fuck you'. You'll feel a lot better.

We Are All Addicts

I now want to touch on the topic of addiction and why we focus so much more on it when it's linked to so-called 'vices'.

Here's a list:

- Sex
- Gambling
- Drink
- Drugs
- Tobacco

Here's another list:

- Food
- Work
- Video games
- Internet
- Coffee
- Sport

Now I appreciate that neither of these lists are exhaustive, they're not meant to be, but they are viewed in a completely different manner when presented to a stranger.

If you went to an interview and they asked you if there was anything medical that they should know about and you said you were addicted to coffee, I've no doubt the reaction would be, 'That's not a problem, we have a Starbucks in the cafeteria.'

If you said that you were addicted to alcohol, they wouldn't say, 'No problem, Mr Kerrison, The Lamb and Flag is only a few metres from the office, and they do a fabulous Merlot!'

The truth is you probably wouldn't get the job.

Now I know the lifestyle damage caused by drinking twenty mochaccinos a day compared to a bottle of vodka may seem uncomparable, but it's the same behavioral problem, the repetition of an action regardless of the consequences.

The fact is, we are all addicts in some way or another. Each of us has addictive behaviour. It may not be destructive – it could be that every time you have a cup of tea you simply must have a biscuit with it – but it is a repetitive action that mentally you find hard to stop.

How many people do you know who spend all their time working and can't manage their work-life balance? Is it the job, is it really? Or is it their choice to put that behaviour before anything else?

How many people do you know who exercise relentlessly or spend their entire life cleaning? I know lots.

I believe addiction is closely linked to routine and that it's no surprise so many people get addicted to things. The repeated action of doing what they do becomes so ingrained in their behaviour, that it becomes very difficult to stop, whatever 'it' may be.

It's not surprising that people get addicted to drink and/or drugs. I believe we have to stop looking at addiction as a dirty word.

Being a drink or drug addict isn't something to destroy your life over. You simply got involved in repetitive behaviour and it became an addiction for you, just like exercise, food or video games for other people.

The problem with addiction is that it's nearly always self-destructive. If you ask yourself the honest question, 'Would I be better off if I didn't do this?' and your answer is yes, then it's probably time to do something about it.

The great thing is that if you do decide to do something about it, I believe anyone can overcome addiction. We can all learn to change our behaviour, and when we do the results can be staggering.

I don't think there's anybody on the planet to have overcome an addiction who sits back after a few years and says, 'What a fucking waste of time that was – ship me back to hell!'

That's not to say you won't think about your addiction; you will. In fact, you'll think about it a lot. But I maintain that anybody who wants to change, can.

The first thing you must do is admit that you have a problem.

Be brave, stop hiding it, grow a pair of massive balls and speak up. It doesn't matter who you tell; trust me, they'll know anyway (even if they haven't already told you they know).

My wife was the first person I told. She already knew that things were well out of control. It was a huge relief. It wasn't easy, but it was the first step – the hardest step, but the most important.

I was honest, told her the situation, admitted I was at rock bottom.

How did it go, you might ask?

It was like a weight off my shoulders, finally the truth was out, and when you're at the bottom, there is only one direction you can go. Up.

How Do You Know if You Have a Problem?

This may sound like a fucking stupid question, but trust me, it isn't.

Let's start with the big one, my dear old friend, Mr Denial.

When I was drinking and taking drugs, I could think of a million reasons as to why I did not have a problem. The best and most common one is comparing yourself to others. You always know someone who drinks more than you, someone who takes more drugs than you and you use them to rationalise your own behaviour. I don't drink as much as X therefore I can't have a problem with drink, they are the one with the issues. I don't spend £1,000 a week on coke like celebrities do, so I must be fine.

Any comparison that would convince me I didn't have a problem, I'd latch onto like the hottest girl at the school dance.

I never drank in the morning (well, mostly never). Boom! Clearly not got a problem. Carry on boozing.

I only do coke in the daytime on a Friday. That's perfectly under control then.

I haven't had a drink for two days, clearly no issues with alcohol for me. I shall now drink two bottles of wine. On a Tuesday.

You see, us problem drink and drug users are exceptionally good at lying to ourselves. There's *always* someone else in a worse state than you, so you compare yourself to them and everything is just fine and fucking dandy.

You'll also find you spend time with people who are happy to partake in and fuel your habits. These are the people who will be disappointed when you stop. They're the people who will have been helping you to stay very good pals with Mr Denial. They will suggest you should maybe just calm it down a bit, go easy, have a break. Secretly they won't want you to stop as it could highlight their own problems or mean they'll lose a drinking or drug-taking buddy.

All along, they'll have been encouraging your denial. It's not necessarily their fault, but I guarantee this will be true. Even when you stop, they will keep helping you deny the issue. You will hear comments such as 'When are you going to stop this ridiculous not drinking shit?' and 'You're not planning on stopping forever, are you?' which do not help at all.

You'll need to have an answer for these people and you might even have tough decisions to make about who you spend time with after you've stopped.

How else do you know that you've got an issue? Here are some of my favourites.

You do it on your own

I didn't need company to drink or take drugs. Truth be told, there were times I preferred to do it on my own. I could go at my own pace, no one was there to tell me what I was doing was wrong and there was no one to tell me when to stop.

However, these are also all the reasons it escalated for me. I had no off switch, I became secretive and often hid my consumption.

If you are drinking or taking drugs alone this is a massive warning signal, particularly when it comes to booze as this can so easily be normalised. I'm not talking about one beer or a glass of wine in the garden from time to time, but if you're getting home, opening a bottle of wine and drinking it all by yourself then alarm bells should be ringing. People with no issue simply do not do this, and however you want to dress it up this is not normal drinking.

You take offence when anyone suggests that you're doing too much

I remember the occasions my wife would tell me I'd drunk enough. That would rile me. I would sit there full of anger thinking that I didn't grow up to be an adult only to be told what to do.

It would be the same if people told me to slow down on a night out. My immediately thought would be, 'Fuck you, I'll do what I want!'

My mother would also make comments from time to time, but I would dismiss them and justify myself with arguments why my drinking was perfectly under control. Sadly, she was right.

You think you have an issue

The reality is, if you think you have an issue, then you do. Towards the end I carried on, but deep down I knew my drinking and drug taking was out of control. I knew it and the reality was that everyone else knew it too.

You plan your week around drinking

Yes, coke was a problem for me, but it was always accompanied by drinking. I would plan my week around the nights I could drink and/or take drugs.

What started with just weekends and my midweek treat, known as 'wankered Wednesdays' (a habit which rolled over from my university days and never stopped), became a pretty much daily occurence. I managed the odd night off, but I was only fooling myself – it was simply the catalyst to get even more smashed the following one.

When it came to the weekend, there was no question, I would drink on Friday, Saturday and, during the latter stages, Sunday nights.

I often remember trying to work out when the last weekend was that I hadn't got drunk or taken cocaine. The reality was there weren't any. It was as simple as that. My weekends meant drink and drugs. Fuck the consequences, fuck the children, fuck any plans for the mornings; it was all about me. It was all about getting smashed. That was my 'fun', there was nothing else. Yes, much of the time it was social, my wife and I often had people round and we would enjoy ourselves with company, but it was *every* weekend, without fail.

Saturday mornings were a wasted haze of being hungover, feeling like shit and doing everything I could to do as little

My Observations

as possible. But that's normal, right? That's what everyone does? Get fucked at the end of the week and recover on the weekends?

No, it's not. There is a whole other world out there on Saturday mornings and it's not just for old people who smell of cabbage and like to get their shopping done early.

Drinking was ingrained in me. How many meetings, presentations, seminars did I attend, feeling like shit because I'd got drunk the night before? Anxiety through the fucking roof, sweating, massively dehydrated and wishing the day to be over.

I wasted so much time in those situations. So many missed opportunities because I wasn't fit for work. I am timid by nature and this just held me back even more. I used to turn up to client meetings still fucked and frankly petrified.

Why had I done this to myself ... again.

Work events in the week. I would get fucked. Every. Single. Time.

On some occasions I'd turn up to the seminar, meeting or presentation not just hungover, but still drunk and stinking of booze. This had the opposite effect. My shyness would disappear, I would 'pipe up', talking shit, arguing over points that didn't matter, being the dick that everyone hates.

When I sit back and reflect on those times, I am so glad it's over. Do you have any idea how good it feels to be able to write that? No? Trust me, you will. Follow my plan and you will.

Drinking and taking drugs were everything to me – week night, weekend, it just did not matter. If I could get away with drinking and snorting coke, I would.

If any of this is ringing true to you, you need to sort yourself out. Trust me, you do.

You can, it's possible and this book will help you.

You hide it

Your immediate thought here is going to be about stashing empty bottles in hidden cupboards, only to clean them out when nobody's looking. Or it might be the whisky in the coffee mug classic, the hip flask at work. These measures are extreme, and you may be doing them, but hiding your habits can be done in more subtle ways.

I've mentioned this already but the recycling bin is a prime example.

If I were a doctor or therapist and someone came to me with signs of alcohol problems and I suspected they were lying about their consumption, I know what I'd do.

I'd dress up as a binman and head to their house on recycling collection day.

Have you ever counted the bottles you throw away over the week? Probably not. I never did either because I knew it would be fucking horrific. The weight of the bin alone told me so. Kilos of clinking glass pointing the finger at my massive booze consumption.

My trick was to take the bin out at midnight when no one was around. I'd stagger across the lawn trying to be as quiet as possible. Bottles would fall and then I'd have to rearrange them in the overflowing bin like those people who stack stones on the beach. I am sure that binmen and women around the world could point to every household with a drinking problem.

Doubling up at the bar was another a favourite of mine. I'd get a round in, making sure I'd order a neat Scotch first. I would then neck it whilst the other drinks were being poured. Clever!

I would often be locked 'n' loaded with extra strong mints and Paco Rabanne to hide the smell of booze. I was probably consuming seven packets of mints a week and dousing myself in cologne on a regular basis. This was mainly in the morning if I had to attend a tightly-packed meeting and I was concerned that the residue of last night's booze may be lingering. I'm sure most people have had to do this on at least one occasion, but when it becomes a necessity on a near daily basis, you know it's not right.

The simple fact of lying about your consumption is hiding it. I'm not talking about the cheeky white lie when you've been to the pub with your mate and had three pints, but tell your wife you only had two. No, I mean the real lying.

This was a common one for me. If my wife went out, I'd drink a bottle of red wine and then open another. I'd discard the first one in the recycling bin, or if I thought she might look there, I'd bury it in the normal bin.

Then I'd try to claim that I'd only had half a bottle of wine, when I'd actually drunk one and a half. She is no fool and if I felt that I wasn't going to get away with it, I would be honest, despite the guaranteed telling off that would incur.

Another sneaky move I'd pull off would be to drink my wife's wine. I'd tell her I wanted to taste her white wine, see if it was any good. Taste? Massive glass more like. Then I was onto my own wine, already a glass in. Smart shit that.

The reality is you don't have to be hiding empty bottles to have a problem. If you're trying to hide how much you're drinking, for any reason, the likelihood is you are already on a slippery slope. I was on that slope, with skis on and a rocket pack.

You can't stop at one drink

Having one drink to me was the biggest waste of time on earth. One glass? One? What will that do? Fuck that.

Quite seriously, there would be occasions, mainly at lunchtime where I would not drink at all because I knew it would only be one and I could not see the point.

The old expression that one is too many and ten is not enough was so true in my case. If I had one, I wanted ten. I wanted to feel drunk. That was the goal, that was the pot of gold at the end of the rainbow. One drink? 'Oh, but you can savour the taste.' Why? I just want to get pissed and be a prick, now hand me that pint!

I couldn't moderate and, as I've said before, people who can moderate don't think about moderation. I thought about it all the time, but just could not do it. Then I would bullshit myself with such twaddle as one bottle of wine a day could be considered moderation.

Trust me, if you're having to consciously think about moderation, you are a problem drinker. End of. No discussion.

My wife can have just one drink. It will take her about half an hour to drink it. When it's finished, she may have one more, but it will only be if she has time before dinner, or if we have friends round. This will be a maximum of once or twice a week.

How does she do that? Not have another drink? Simple. It doesn't cross her mind.

It's all about the mind. It would have crossed my mind many times about having another drink, in fact it would no doubt have been crossing it from about 4 p.m.

Sadly, if you're a problem drinker, you cannot just have one drink. It will not work.

You will be tempted, you may even succumb, but I guarantee you will never just be able to have one or two glasses. I believe most problem drinkers are back to their pre-sobriety status within two weeks of falling off the wagon. In some cases, it can be one day.

You simply must stay off it. Abstinence is the only way. Yeah, it's a fucker, but it's the truth.

It is your hobby

There were times during job interviews or when meeting new people on an evening out that the question of what I do in my spare time would be asked.

I would always have to lie. I'd come up with some shit about mountain biking, cars or even fucking cooking, but the honest answer to this question was simple: 'I like to get off my tits on booze and coke.'

I never had the balls to say it, of course, but if this were the answer you would give to this question, if you were really honest, then you know you have a problem.

Your health is suffering

Apart from the shits, I used to get a pain in my lower back after a big night out. I believe it was around the kidney region, but for someone who thought a 'tibia' was a type of fish, I could easily be wrong.

It would ache in a dull sort of way, and I knew this was due to the booze. I never got it checked out and it has since gone away, but I'm sure it was a warning sign.

Most people will probably ignore them, as did I, but if you're drinking too much, you know why the pain is there. You have been warned.

You drink even when you don't really feel like drinking.

This may sound crazy, but there were times when I really didn't feel like I could face a drink. These instances were not frequent but they mostly occurred the night after big drinking sessions or if I had been drinking every night for a few days.

The trouble was, even if I didn't feel like I wanted a drink, I would believe that I'd feel better if I did. There'd also be the outside pressure from other people, 'Go on, have a drink, it'll sort you out!'

This still makes me laugh. I mean how many times have you heard this in your life?

I always wondered what would happen if I turned up to a dinner party and said that I wasn't feeling that great, I won't be drinking, but I did have half a gram of cocaine in my pocket and that that might help.

Would the response be, 'Go on, get a line up your hooter, you'll feel better for it!' I doubt it. In fact, the reaction would probably be, 'You're not doing drugs in my house, get out!'

Funny that. The difference I mean. I mean, is there a difference? How do you discriminate between one highly addictive and destructive drug that's legal and the other highly addictive and destructive drug that isn't? I guess the answer's in the question – one is against the law, the other isn't. Think about it.

Anxiety

Here I must make an apology. I can't write much about anxiety because I never really suffered from it that badly. However, I know for some of you it is devastating.

My main experiences of anxiety would be following a big weekend. The Monday would be hell, particularly after drugs. Occasionally I would be a shaking mess, wrecked with the guilt of having got so fucked over the weekend and with no way to shake it, other than the best tool of them all, more booze and drugs.

I don't know if you can call this anxiety, or if it was real anxiety, but I am convinced alcohol and drugs fuelled it. I would feel scared about things, particularly in terms of work and anything important that I had to do. Although I am sure that if you genuinely suffer from anxiety, there is no way drinking or taking drugs is going to help in any way at all.

In terms of what I sensed as anxiety, all I can say is that in my experience, many of the fears, worry and concerns I faced when hungover or down completely disappeared when I quit.

I think that pretty much covers it. In addition to getting fat and disrupted sleep, which I mentioned earlier, this pretty exhaustively covers all my observations on addiction from my own experience.

I've no doubt you will have been nodding in agreement through many of these points and hopefully I've provided some insight into what we all go through. The key message is that you are not alone – these habits and issues are experienced by millions of people all over the world who are all going through the same thing.

If you recognise yourself in these, even if you resonate with just some of the points, then you probably need a way out and the good news is that I'm going to share this with you now. I'll focus on how I hauled myself out of addiction, the steps I took, the plans I made. And through this, I hope to provide you with the tools you need to change your life and get sober.

Let's go.

CHAPTER 4
GETTING SOBER

Make Your Decision

So here we get to the part of the book where I'm done telling you what I think. My story has been told and now you must decide if you want to do anything about yours.

If there are any parts of this book so far you can relate to, sections where you think 'that's me', then you have an issue. But let's be honest, you wouldn't be reading this if you didn't.

What I wanted to do in the first three chapters was to get across all the subjects I picked up on during my drinking and drug career and the feelings I've had about them since quitting. I wanted to share them in the hope that they offer some connection, hope and reassurance that what you're going through is an experience that many, many people go through.

There are a lot of us out there, going through the same shit. The vast majority of us want out, and I'm sure you do too.

The good news is there is a way.

Not a day goes by when I don't feel grateful to be sober. Sure, I'm no longer part of that other club, but frankly it was a club that fucked me up.

Getting sober requires two things. A decision and a plan.

You must remember that very few people succeed in something the first-time round. How many Formula One drivers won their first race in an F1 car? None.

What is common though, with every person I've met who's made significant change to their lives, is they made their decision, formulated a plan around it, and stuck to it.

How are you going to get from where you are now, to where you want to be?

What does success look like, and how do you keep being successful?

What I'm going to go through now is what I did. It's what worked for me. It is not a definitive 'How to give up drinking and drugs in fifty days' bullshit program, it is advice. However, I guarantee that if you take some of these ideas and put them into your plan, they will help you to succeed.

The first thing, and I know I keep repeating this, is that you need to want to get sober.

Not for your partner, not for your kids, not because you think you should, not because it will buy you some time until you can start using again, not to get the subject off the table. No, none of that shit. This needs to be you making the biggest decision you have ever made in your life. For yourself.

The difference between the first time I tried to stop and failed, and the second time was that I wanted it. I wanted it more than I wanted to carry on. I had a deep desire to find out what life could be without drink and drugs. I wanted this more than anything else. I wanted a new life and I knew this was the only way to get it.

And you know what? Once I made the decision, something very strange happened. I felt proud and excited about the future. I knew I was at the beginning of an exhilarating journey – I had the chance to do something different and the way to do it could be very simple.

Stop drinking and taking drugs and everything will get better.

Stop drinking and taking drugs and everything will get better.

Stop drinking and taking drugs and everything will get better.

That's it. That's the decision you must make.

Do *you* want everything to get better? Do you really, really, more than anything else in your whole life, want things to get better?

If your answer is yes, and I mean a real yes, a yes with conviction that there is nothing that's going to stop you achieving this, and not a 'yes, I can try this' or a 'yes, let's see how for this goes', but a 'yes, I am going to change', then you have completed step one.

You give a fuck. You are going to do something about it.

Well done.

I'm proud of you and so will everybody you know be. Including yourself.

Decide if You Need Professional Help

I did not seek professional help, but I did think about it. A lot, in fact.

I considered Alcoholics Anonymous but didn't take it any further. The reason being, I felt that for me it was just too big a step. The name alone put me off. It was like admitting that I was too far gone to be saved and I personally didn't see myself as an alcoholic, even though technically I was.

I knew I had an issue, that I was a problem drinker, but I almost felt that to go to one of these meetings would be a walk of shame. I also, probably stupidly, feared the impact it would have on me when having to tell people that I was going to AA.

I worried that people would judge me, whispering in other people's ears at parties.

'You know he's an alcoholic, he attends AA.'

'Oh really, how terrible!'

AA and NA (Narcotics Anonymous) for that matter are not terrible. They're incredible support structures that have helped thousands of people beat their demons. According to an article published in Stanford Medicine by Mandy Erickson, The AA model — open to all and free — has spread around the globe, and AA now boasts over 2 million members in 180 nations and more than 118,000 groups. When adhered to, their twelve step programs work and they are a great place to get help. Do just not dismiss them because I did. If you want to seek, or need, medical help, then please use the traditional routes of your doctor and well-established organisations for dealing with your problems. They are there to help you. But for me I felt that there must be other ways to get guidance.

We live in a world of technology, where help is at our fingertips. AA was established in 1935 and, whilst I am sure it has evolved, I wanted a more modern approach.

I wanted to access help from home, in my own time. I wanted to find people who I could connect to, those people out there who were just like me.

It didn't take long to find them.

If you want to hear other people's experiences, understand how they did it and get tips and updates every day, then the Internet is your friend. I'm only able to tell you about how I personally stopped drinking and taking drugs. Community-based support is so key, but these days you can get it without stepping foot in any clinic, centre or doctor's surgery.

The tool that helped me from day one – and still helps me now – is YouTube.

YouTube has been incredible. You see there is a whole community of people that you have probably never heard of who post regular videos to help the likes of you and me. They are brilliant.

My curiosity actually started before I had made my decision. I'd been aware for a while that my downfall was coming. So, I started looking shit up on YouTube; you know, stuff like, 'How to quit drinking', 'Am I an alcoholic?', 'Is two bottles of wine too much?'

I found various channels that answered all my questions almost without looking. It was like opening a door to find a group of people who all looked exactly like me. I couldn't believe it. I wasn't alone. You aren't either.

It is unbelievable just how many people have been through exactly the same shit as you and me.

I suddenly found this wealth of information that had me going 'that's me', 'yeah, I did that shit'. 'You describe yourself as a problem drinker? Fuck! Me too!'

What's even better about it is that the content doesn't stop when you walk out of the room or leave the clinic. At the beginning, my workday would commence with me watching ten minutes of YouTube videos on not drinking. In the evening, I could dip into a quick clip whenever I started thinking about drink or drugs.

The support is there constantly, 24/7. I still regularly watch videos today.

It also helped in another way, it made me feel a bit special. You see, many of these people haven't just quit, but they've gone onto achieve great things. Some of the motivational talks and speeches are truly incredible. It makes you want some of that too. I can honestly say, hand on heart, that the following people helped me quit drink and drugs. They have motivated me to be a better person, they have improved everything in my life. They don't know that they helped me, but maybe they will now. Here they are for your viewing pleasure:

Kevin O'Hara – *Habits V2*

Craig Beck – *Stop Drinking Expert*

Marcus and Terry – *Talk Sober*

Annie Grace – *This Naked Mind* (also the author of a book of the same name)

Paul Churchill – TEDx Talks, 'I've been duped by alcohol'

Clare Pooley – TEDx Talks, 'Making sober less shameful' (also the author of *The Sober Diaries*)

Joe Rogan Experience – this channel is full of no holds barred videos about drugs and alcohol and the destruction they bring

Chris Herren, a former Celtics basketball player who overcame drug addiction – TEDx Talks, *The game has changed*

This is just a small selection – there are many more – but each of these helped me a great deal. You need to find what's right for you; see whose advice you like and follow them.

I also found podcasts to be a good source of information and great for when you're in the car. Again, you can search these out for yourself, but here are the main ones I tune in to.

David Boyle – *I'm Quitting Alcohol* – an utterly brilliant 5-minute daily podcast

James Swanwick – *Alcohol-Free Lifestyle* – great advice on all aspects of living a healthy lifestyle

Kate and Mandy – *Love Sober Podcast* – two friends, one of whom lives in France, the other in the UK, chat about the benefits and stories of sobriety

Now onto books. I read the following books and they were all excellent.

Allen Carr (yes, he's the cigarette bloke) – *Stop Drinking Now*
Clare Pooley – *The Sober Diaries*
Annie Grace – *This Naked Mind*

There are plenty of fantastic books out there. I would thoroughly recommend buying some (like you bought this one) as they will give you other people's perspectives, stories, plans and advice.

It's about finding the nuggets of information that work for you. Finding those authors that inspire you. This is a select and special community which means that you can often directly contact authors via blogs or YouTube channels and they generally take the time to reply.

I don't know of any YouTuber or blogger who talks or writes about this subject who doesn't want to help. It's their raison d'être and all of us are here to assist anyone who wants it. If we can change people's lives for the better, then it's all been worthwhile.

There is a whole world of support waiting for you out there. You are not alone and, with the Internet, you need never be.

Go search, watch, read and listen. It works.

Create Your Plan

Nothing was ever constructed without a plan and no long-term plan was ever successful without writing something down. Even the A-Team must have occasionally made notes to ensure a plan came together.

You're about to change the way you live your life. It's a simple as that. Suddenly you're going to have time to fill. Drinking and taking drugs combats boredom, it's something to do and it's no doubt how you've been using your free time for many years. Taking into account the physical act of consuming, being fucked and getting over being fucked, you can waste hours, days, weeks, even lifetimes.

Put quite simply, you must replace that time with other things. If you don't, you will get bored and I can tell you exactly where boredom is going to lead you.

It's not easy, I know. I remember a few years back my dad picked me up on my drinking and told me I needed a hobby of some sort. At the time, I was like, 'Fuck that!' and to be honest, I still don't have a hobby per se.

I'm not one of those people to suddenly take up pottery or enrol in Mandarin classes. However, if that's your thing, do it.

My plan was simpler, and it started with the first month.

I knew that to be successful, I had to be occupied for those first four weeks. I needed to go back to a school timetable routine. Not for every hour of the day, but for those hours where I would normally drink or take coke – mainly the evenings and weekends.

Oddly, the cinema was my salvation. I've always loved films and there are many I like to watch that my wife doesn't (no, not porn).

On day one, I went to the cinema and signed up for a pass so I could watch as many films as I wanted, when I wanted.

I would purposely go to the later showings, 9.30 p.m. ish so that I could come home after work, have dinner and then go to a movie. Yes, I would go on my own. That might sound a bit sad, but I didn't give a fuck, and it's surprising how many people do go to the cinema on their own.

I would buy myself some pick 'n' mix – I fucking love sweets and when you give up booze your body definitely craves sugar, nothing that a big bag of cola bottles, strawberry laces and jelly babies can't sort out. I didn't feel guilty about it and neither should you. Pretty much everyone I know who has stopped booze gets this sugar craving and my view is that if you suddenly want to scoff three donuts and a Twix, fucking go for it. You're off the booze and that's what counts. The rest will fall into line as you progress.

Cake is the one for me. Fuck me do I like cake. Never cared for it much before, now I fucking purr over a Swiss Roll.

It wasn't just the cinema though. It was planning things with my kids – board game nights, movie nights, going for walks in the evening, anything to disrupt my old thought patterns and lifestyle habits.

On that first day, I took a piece of paper and filled every evening with an activity. It was Blu Tacked to a cupboard door in my bedroom for the whole family to see, and I stuck to it religiously.

The weekends were all about the kids. Holy shit did they benefit! Not just from the obvious point of having a Dad who was no longer fucked or hungover, no, I built my weekends around them. I gave them their Daddy back.

They have never been to as many theme parks, McDonald's and toy shops as they did in that first month.

Expensive you may say? Not a scratch on what I had been spending on booze and drugs. We had fun and we became a proper family. One where fun is not induced but lived. And that fun continues every day of my life now (well, not the theme parks).

You must plan what you're going to do. I appreciate some of you don't have families or kids, but that doesn't stop you taking a sheet of paper, writing out the days of the week and putting in things that you want and can do.

Here's what the first two weeks of mine looked like.

Week 1						
Mon	Tues	Wed	Thurs	Fri	Sat	Sun
YouTube Videos (10 mins before work)	YouTube Videos (10 mins before work)	Go for Run	YouTube Videos (10 mins before work)	Read sober blogs	Go for Run	Go for Run
Work	Work	Work	Work	Work	Visit family	Restaurant and Walk
Bike ride with kids	Cinema night	Movie night with Kids	Take away meal night	Board game night	Watch Series with Wife	Movie night with kids

Week 2						
Mon	Tues	Wed	Thurs	Fri	Sat	Sun
YouTube Videos (10 mins before work)	Go for Run	YouTube Videos (10 mins before work)	Read sober blogs	YouTube Videos (10 mins before work)	Go for Run	Go for Run
Work	Work	Work	Work	Work	Toy shopping with kids	Picnic in park
Cinema night	Movie night with Kids	Board game night	Cooking night with kids	Family meal at restaurant	Movie night	Plan holiday

What you must be clear about is that you don't have to stop living. Do not lock yourself in the house, do go out. Another thing I found great was going for a meal. Not a swanky restaurant with a tempting wine list, but just a meal, with a friend or family member. Tell the person when you arrive that you're not drinking. Enjoy the food and use it as time to talk if you need.

I always found that once I'd eaten my desire to drink diminished. So, another recommendation would be is to plan to eat early. When I drank, it was the total opposite. Why? Because eating would simply get in the way of drinking. If you came to my house on a Friday night when I was drinking, you would never eat before 11 p.m. In fact, I'm pretty sure that some of my friends turned down nights at mine due to this.

Get pissed, get more pissed, then when we really must, have some food. And that's if I did eat. When I was on coke, I would literally have to force it down. Cocaine suppresses the appetite like nothing else. Eating was an almighty effort. Drinking on the other hand was not.

Another thing to consider in your plan is who you are not going to see.

If drugs are your problem, the dealer's phone numbers must go. This is easier said than done. I can remember on numerous occasions having sworn that I wouldn't do cocaine again, deleting all my dealer's numbers only to look them up via my phone bill a week later. There's also the issue of them contacting you. You might receive the odd text message to remind you they're still around, or even some tempting 2 for 1 deals (yes they do exist!)

With drugs it's tough, because in general your dealer is not necessarily your friend. You rarely hang out with them and whilst you can ask them to remove your number and stop texting you, it's quite possible that they won't.

In this case there are two options. First, you could change your number. Get a new number and never put theirs in your phone again. Or secondly, exert all your self-discipline and delete the numbers. They'll stop bothering you eventually, and drug dealers tend to change their phone often, so unless they text you the new number and you save it, you will soon have the wrong contact details for them.

I chose option 2.

The reality is, if you really want to get their number back, you'll find a way. Once again, it comes back to your decision – do you really want to stop all this shit or not?

In terms of your old drinking buddies, you must simply steer clear of them at the beginning.

In fact, quitting drink and/or drugs really does sort out who are your friends and who is just an acquaintance. Trust me, this is no bad thing. Why spend time with people who you *think* like you, when you can live a life with those who really *do* like you. They are the ones who will stay with you, support you and enjoy being with you as you embark on your new life.

Seriously, get rid of the dross. Fuck 'em! You don't need any bad apples, particularly at the beginning; leave that tree well alone, Adam.

What if you live with people who are going to tempt you? This is tricky, no doubt. However, if a sensible conversation can't sort things out (maybe your partner is also a problem drinker or drug taker) then you really need to question why you're living with that person in the first place.

If you need to, move out. Go back to Mum and Dad, stay at a friend's house, whatever works for you. No one will mind, it will not be embarrassing, and you will not be considered a failure for doing this. If you want this, I mean really want this, your real friends will always open their doors for you.

In summary, get rid of the phone numbers, avoid those that will lead you into temptation and if you need, move out to a place where you cannot be led astray.

Tell People (Or Not)

There are two schools of thought here. The first being to shout it from the rooftops. You tell all your family and your friends about your decision and get it out there immediately. The alternative is to keep it more personal. You only tell those close to you until you feel comfortable with your story and achieve a sustained period of sobriety.

There are arguments for both.

The decision to quit drink and/or drugs is a big one and no doubt something that many of you will want to share with other people. By announcing this to all, you will no doubt get some wonderful feedback and immense support from all those who know you. Some want it this way, others don't.

For some, you will want to go further and announce your decision on Instagram, Snapchat or TikTok. You may feel that by telling the world it will give you the drive and desire to get and stay sober. The sharing of your journey on social media can also help some people as it gives them a large platform of support during potentially tough times when you may question your sobriety.

The downside of this is you may be putting unnecessary pressure on yourself. What if you 'slip up', what if you don't get sober the first time around? How do you deal with that message? It really depends on what sort of person you are. Me? I chose the second option and I'll tell you why.

You see, I was scared of failure. Yes, I had made my decision, but drink and drugs were so ingrained in me that they had become my identity. It is very hard to change your identity immediately, and I wanted to make sure that I truly had before announcing that fact to the world.

It took me well over a year before I posted on Facebook that I was sober.

I guess you could say I simply wanted to be completely sure before telling the world that I was now a changed man.

I was concerned that I may fail or slip up. I did the first time and, for this reason, I didn't want to say, 'Look at me, I have sorted out all my problems!' only to have to tell everyone that I'd had a setback.

I say setback, because if you've made the decision to stop, that's all it will be. Trust me, in most cases the guilt you will feel when you fall off the wagon will be enough for you to get straight back on it, sat up front, stroking the horses.

At the very beginning, I only told my wife. Then, a few weeks in I told my immediate family and friends. I could have made the big announcement to everyone else before a year had passed, after all it was already very clear in my mind that I would never go back to drink and drugs, but twelve months felt like a significant timeframe, so I waited until then.

I don't dwell on the actual date of my last drink or drug. It's just not something I need to think about, and I don't really care. As I am writing this now It's been just over four years, but the specific date for me is not significant. For some though, it's very important to know the date, to have that precise reminder. I also totally understand that for certain people, it is much better to lay all their cards on the table from day one and announce to the world what they are doing. I like that, it's brave.

All I would say is that you should think about this before reacting. I will hold my hand up and say perhaps my approach was in some ways to cover any potential diversions back to the booze or drugs, but it worked out well for me because I was so committed to the decision I'd made.

Another aspect you need to be aware of when you first get sober is that there is a honeymoon phase.

When you first stop, there will be a period of euphoria. This will come from within and will be supported by those around you telling you how wonderful and amazing you are. Sadly, it will wear off. Not completely, certainly not from yourself. I still feel fucking proud of what I've achieved, but people will eventually stop saying how great you look, how much weight you've lost, how much brighter your skin is. After time, your new you will become the normal you.

This is why some people choose to document their journey from day one. It allows them to keep the focus on their sobriety and as long as they have relevant content, they can keep going and it can be very helpful to themselves and others.

But you must be aware of this honeymoon period. It's like everything, it becomes the norm. But trust me, the norm is so much better than the chaos. Embrace the norm!

The choice is yours. It's up to you to choose how you want to tell people and the approach you want to take. There is not a 'best' method, no silver bullet. You should consider the options I've set out, their possible consequences and decide which will work best for you.

Prepare Your Elevator Speech

For those of you who are unfamiliar with the concept of an elevator speech, it is the idea that if you got into a lift (elevator in the US) and someone asked you about an idea, product or company, you could explain it in the short time that it takes the lift to go to the floor you or they have selected and in such a way that anyone can understand it.

The reason you're going to need an elevator speech when you decide to get sober is you're going to regularly find yourself in situations where you'll be offered the drug you've given up, refuse it and then be required to explain why.

I'll be honest, it can be a fucking pain in the arse. So you'd better be ready with a speech or, as in my case, several speeches.

Your response will depend on many things. Who is offering you the booze or drug? Where you are – are you at a work event or someone's house? How much do you want to tell the person asking the question? How brave are you feeling? Do you want to lie? (There is nothing wrong with lying in certain situations if you'd prefer.) The list goes on.

Alcohol is the hardest as it will be offered to you constantly, and to make matters worse some people won't take no for an answer. 'Go on, it's champagne, you've got to have a drink!' was a recent one for me and even though I kept saying no, this phrase was repeated several times. I remember it well. I was at a work event and I didn't really want to tell someone I hardly knew that I had drug and alcohol issues and abstained from all substances, including champagne. Fortunately she gave up after the third attempt and swiftly fucked off.

So, what can you say when someone offers you a drink or the inevitable wine glass is placed in front of you at a dinner or party?

My line tends to be simple, classic and direct: 'No thanks, I don't drink.' and then see what the response is. Or sometimes, given that I live in France, I may jokingly say that I am one of the very few English people who doesn't like a drink (we have a reputation, the Brits are known to be big drinkers and to be fair we do wear that reputation quite well, at least I certainly did). I don't go into detail unless I am asked why and even then, I will adapt my speech to the person I'm dealing with.

The majority of the time, if pushed, I will say that I used to drink, but decided I was done with it. If pressed further, I will add that I found it was getting in the way of the things I wanted to do and I wanted to see what life was like without alcohol. I always finish by saying, 'My life is a million times better without alcohol.'

The best bit about delivering your elevator speech is the reaction you get from people. Quite often it's, 'Oh I'm sorry!', sometimes, 'That's a shame', and you even get the odd, 'Sounds like a boring life to me!'

However, it's what happens afterwards that can be very interesting. It often sparks open debate about the pros and cons of giving up booze; a mini-AA meeting can occur with you as the focal point. The reality is I've never had a problem with this, and it can be quite fun as people become intrigued about what life is like after booze (and drugs, should the conversation be taken there).

Sometimes, it can go even further. I have had the odd person quietly come up to me and ask for help either for themselves or someone they know. When this happens, I tend to tell them the full story, no holds barred. This then becomes one of the most rewarding situations a sober person can experience, the ability to share your story and possibly help someone else who is going through the same hell that you did.

This is why I've written this book. I don't consider myself a writer and I'm not in this for the money. I'm just a man who got sober, turned his life around and wants to share his story to help others do the same. Simple.

I will say something else too, I know damn well who else needs my help. They may never want it, but if they do, they know where to find me. So will you.

What you also must understand is your elevator speech or speeches are going to have to be wheeled out for the rest of your life. Even now, one of my wonderful friends whom I love dearly will often forget and offer me a drink. Then they quickly remember that I don't. 'Matt, glass of ... oh no, fuck, you can't, that's a shame, sorry!'

But it doesn't matter one bit, because when you get sober and you're content with it, you're not sorry, you're fucking delighted.

In short, have the answers you're happy with, be open and honest if you want or, if you prefer to lie, then do so. 'I have a medical condition, can't drink, yeah it's a fucker.' But be prepared, especially at the beginning, because you will get offered and you will have to say no.

To conclude, a quick nod to my old friend cocaine. I have not been offered it since I quit. It is also the type of drug, possibly due to the amount it costs, where if the question were popped, a simple 'Nah, you're alright mate' ('No, thank you' in British street talk) would suffice, no further questions asked.

Do the Work

Sean Whalen is a father, entrepreneur, public speaker, podcaster, business coach and the founder the Lions Den, a premiere coaching group, and the Lions Not Sheep apparel company. Check it out at www.lionsnotsheep.com

I do not know Whalen, but I have followed him on Facebook, Instagram and read his book *How To Make Sh*t Happen*.

Whalen may not be everyone's cup of tea – he loves guns, speaks his mind and is a true American patriot, but whether you like him or not (I don't think he really gives a fuck either way), he writes about things that resonate with me in a big way.

His journey is one of success to failure, and back to success again. I'm not going to tell his story here, you can look him up, but what I really like about him is that he doesn't mince his words and advocates a very blunt view of what it takes to be successful.

His motto is 'Do the Work'.

I buy into this expression wholeheartedly. He often talks about the difference between those who have achieved in life and those who have not. The distinction is nearly always those who are successful have done the work required to get to where they are.

They don't sit around talking about their dreams or desires, they get off their arses and do something about it. Like him, I too believe that no one has a great family life without putting the effort in, no one gets rich by doing fuck all and no one has a great job by not doing any hard work. No one owes you anything in this life, if you want something you've got to get up and go and get it.

If you want to get sober, you've got to put in the effort. This isn't something that's just going to happen to you because you've decided you should stop drinking. You must do the work to achieve your life-changing event.

How many people do you know who fucking moan about their lives, but aren't willing to put in the work to change them? If you're like me, fucking loads. I know because I was one of them. In most aspects of my life, I wasn't doing the work it took to move my situation forward and make things happen. Getting sober was the first time I really 'did the work' and since then I haven't stopped.

The proof is in the writing of this book, something I could never have envisaged when I was drinking and taking drugs. As I write, on the bottom left corner of my screen there is a cut down Post-it note with three words on it.

Do the Work.

I have accomplished a number of good things since I got sober but, again, these didn't just happen to me. Getting sober allowed me to do the work to achieve them. Sobriety removes the barriers that are holding you back and gives you the time to realise your potential and ultimately, your dreams.

Get into Exercise

I'm not going to beat around the bush here – exercise has been my saviour. I'm not a team sports player and I was fucking hopeless at sport when I was a kid. Honestly, I can't keep a football up in the air for more than two seconds, I spent many a miserable afternoon on the school rugby pitch praying for the game to end, and when it came to athletics, I came last. Every time.

This was not cool when I was a kid. The way that teams were divided for sports practice would be by having two team captains taking alternate picks out of a group of kids to create two teams. Naturally the best ones would be picked first, then it would eventually whittle down to the useless and overweight. In short, me and some porky kid. I was picked last for any team and there were certain kids I simply didn't mix with because sport was their thing, and it wasn't mine. This still goes on in schools and it's utterly humiliating.

Computer games were not my thing either, still aren't, though strangely my son is obsessed with them. I wasn't lazy or wanting to stay indoors all the time, but for me sport and exercise were something that had to be endured and the idea that it could be fun was simply impossible.

It will therefore come as no surprise to hear that as soon as school was over, any form of sport or exercise went completely out of the window. Booze, drugs, girls and cars became my thing and the thought of standing on a cold field kicking any sort of ball around soon became a distant memory.

However, when I reached the age of twenty-five, I decided that to combat my unhealthy lifestyle I should probably get off my arse and do some exercise. I've always been a solitary fellow, so I decided to start running, the perfect sport to do on your own.

At first, I hated it, but then a digital revolution came along. More precisely, the invention of the iPod. I had dicked about with portable CD players, but they were hopeless. Your music would skip and jump constantly, and it meant running with the equivalent of sandwich toaster in your hand.

The iPod changed it all for me. It meant I could run (if you can really call it that at the beginning, trotting would be more apt) with all the music I could ever want in the palm of my hand. I never managed great distances, but I ran at least twice a week.

Since getting sober, this has increased, but fundamentally it has helped me get and stay sober. You may not believe it, but physical activity is one of the best things for your mental health, and I think that running can appeal greatly to problem drinkers or drug takers.

You see, as an addict, I would often drink or use drugs on my own. Not always but given that I would drink almost every night and take cocaine at least once a week, there were many times when I would. As I've already mentioned, it's sometimes better on your own as there's no one to tell you that you shouldn't be doing it, or when to stop – perfect!

Running is the same, it's mostly a solitary exercise. There's no one to tell you how far to run, which way to go, what music to listen to. You choose and you dictate, much like you do when you have an addiction, except that running is good for you.

Another link is the buzz you get from running, or any form of exercise, known as 'runner's high'. The release of endorphins during and after exercise is what make you feel great; you can even experience feelings of euphoria and wellbeing. You may think I'm mad or that this sounds dangerous as it is indeed the same sort of terminology that we use in the drink and drug world, but this is natural and does you no harm.

Yes, you can get addicted to exercise. As I've stated before, I believe everyone is addicted to something (I vape, yeah still not got rid of that one yet), but the reality is exercise is almost always beneficial, unlike booze and drugs.

I truly believe that exercise is key to getting sober. You may not like the sound of it, but you need to try it, sorry, do it (there is no 'try', just 'do'). It doesn't have to be running, it can be anything you like. Yoga, swimming or even a brisk walk are all excellent ways to get active regardless of your level of fitness. Exercise and pleasure will become the new you, maybe not at first, but then was your first ever sip of alcohol pleasurable?

I would also argue that almost every person that has quit drink or drugs now does some form of exercise. It works, it really does, and more importantly it kills time, in a good way. It helps stop the boredom, gives you focus and as you already know, killing the boredom is key to getting off and staying off the poison.

Here's some other wonderful shit exercise does:

- It can help depression and anxiety. I have heard from people who suffer from these (I understand that they are two distinct conditions) who say that working out helps balance your brain's chemistry, takes your mind off stress, boosts your confidence and self-worth, and builds a pattern of resilience that can help you deal with challenging situations. This is no cure, but anything that helps must be worth a mention.
- It gives you energy and increases your resistance to feeling tired. Believe it or not, even though your body is working harder when you exercise, over time,

you feel less tired than you did before you started working out.

- It helps you to lose weight and keep it off. Or as I like to see it, run in the morning, pizza for lunch, not a fucking problem.
- It makes your muscles stronger. You won't turn into He-Man, but you will tone up.
- It's good for your ticker. It helps decrease your risk of heart-related illness.
- It reduces your risk of contracting type 2 diabetes, and for those who already suffer from it can significantly reduce symptoms.
- Honestly, this is not me bigging myself up, but I truly believe I've kept my relatively youthful appearance thanks to exercise. Just go into the street and look at the difference between fit people and unfit people. You can see for yourself.
- It helps you sleep. You burn energy and bring wellbeing to your mind. You will sleep like a baby. (Never understood that expression, my daughter didn't sleep for the first two years.)
- Here's the last one, and I can't believe I am going to say it: Exercise is fun.

To conclude this chapter I want to recap the list I've presented before moving on to some of the things to think about once your journey has begun. I know this is a simple list, but trust me, get this in order, write it down, use it and you will have an excellent plan to help your foray into the incredible world of sobriety.

Make your decision

This decision will be one of, if not the biggest, of your life. You need to make it for yourself and you need to be 100 percent sure it's what you want. If not, you will fail.

Decide if you need professional help

If you feel you do, now's the time to seek it. Use the Internet, speak to your doctor, there is help available for anyone out there who wants it. If you don't feel you need professional help, as was my case, start to get into the YouTube videos or talk to people, you *will* need some form of support. Check out the ones I've mentioned or any others that click with you. Essentially start getting your ducks lined up, as I found a daily dose of support videos or podcasts was essential to my journey.

Create your plan

Write out your plan for the first two weeks of your sobriety (a fortnight minimum; a month is better, but I did four weeks). Schedule your days so the time is filled. You need to know what you're going to be doing every day from when you wake up to when you go to bed. Make sure there are some fun activities in there, even if they cost money (you will be saving a ton on booze and/or drugs so trust me, you'll be able to afford it). If you work, then weekends are particularly important, make sure they're loaded with enjoyable stuff to do. Make sure you communicate your plan to those you live with as they will need to be onboard with everything you do, especially at the beginning.

Tell people (or not)

You need to decide if you want to tell people what you're doing, who you will tell and how. My advice is to keep it to a close group of family and friends at the start. Share your plan with them, talk to them about why you want to stop. Trust me, they will have been worried about you for a long time already, even if they've never said anything before. Talking about your decision is a key step in getting sober. You'll be amazed by the positive reaction and help that close family and friends can offer. It's instant too and will help you do something that you probably haven't done in a very long time – feel good about yourself.

Prepare your elevator speech.

You're going to get the question, it's inevitable. Why don't you drink? It can simply be through intrigue or be more invasive, depending on the person asking. Be ready, plan what you're going to say according to the situation. My advice is, if you're not sure, be honest. Telling the truth is one of the greatest things that comes with sobriety. There's nothing more to hide. It's liberating, truly wonderful and life changing.

Do the work

You must do the work and it's a full-time job to start with. Nothing great comes without effort. Plan well and the effort can even be enjoyable as you rack up the days of sobriety and implement real long-lasting behavioural changes. Think about Jeff Bezos; do you really think it was easy creating Amazon? Do you think it all just fell from the sky and he became the richest person in the world? Of course not. He made a decision, had a plan and did the work. You can achieve anything you want if you are willing to do the work. Achieving sobriety is fucking awesome. I love this quote by Jamie Lee Curtis, to me it says it all:

'Getting sober just exploded my life. Now I have a much clearer sense of myself and what I can and can't do. I am more successful than I have ever been. I feel very positive where I never did before, and I think that's all a direct result of getting sober.'

Get into exercise

Exercise helps. End of. I don't care who you are, how old you are or what shape you're in; if you can get out and exercise, it will help you with sobriety. You don't have to be running 10k on day one, but even if you just go for a walk, get on a bike and cycle somewhere or go to a gym, exercise will help you. I know so many people who have overcome so many things through the routine and wellbeing exercise brings, it must be on your agenda. Don't be afraid, don't worry about what you look like, everyone has their 'day one'. Find a sport or type of exercise that might be enjoyable to you and stick to it. Soon it will become part of your routine and you will even miss not doing it on the days you can't. It can also take you places that you may never normally go. I run around Paris and almost every time discover something new in this wonderful city that I'd never noticed before. Just get up and get out, it doesn't matter what you do, but we all have a body, and you can do amazing things with it, just take a walk at the beginning, that's all that's needed. Get up, get out, breathe deeply, and open your eyes. The world is a beautiful place.

CHAPTER 5

STAYING SOBER

For the next phase, I could just write 'repeat Chapter 4' every day. However, even those of us who get sober and successfully pull our heads out of the shit and into sobriety need to think about how to stay sober. In many ways, writing this book is part of my own staying sober phase.

You see, if you were addicted as I was and you get sober, you're going to experience the end of the honeymoon period. The novelty will wear off, normality will return, and the questions and praise will die down. The problem then becomes the little fuckers in your head who every now and then will want to come up for a little chat. When this happens, you need to be on your game as unfortunately, like many of us before, you might accidently open the door, puff up the cushions, welcome them in and pour out the drinks.

Slipping Up: The Fantasy of Using Again

'You may have to fight a battle more than once to win it' Margaret Thatcher

Let's get this clear right now, slipping up happens. The other term for this is relapse, but I don't like that word. To me it's too brutal, screams failure and in sobriety, there is no failure as long as you keep trying to get sober.

Every single person who has problems with drink or drugs, no matter how bad, will associate good times with their former drink and drug days. I had plenty of them. Fun times, fucked off my tits.

The mind has an incredible ability to focus on the good more than the bad, especially once you've been sober for a while. I'm not a woman so please don't kill me for this, but I can imagine it's like childbirth. Immediately after, you swear that you never want to go through the pain again and two years later, you're back in hospital, legs in the air and in absolute agony.

The reality is that you *will* fantasise about the good times you had. I still do. I had some amazing experiences and I do reminisce about them. I cannot lie, there are occasions when I think how much I would like to go to the pub with some good friends, a gram of coke in my pocket and get properly fucked.

But you must have the counter argument ready in your mind. You must remind yourself of just how much better you are now without all the pain and destruction that came with your problems.

You know the fun times didn't exist at the end and you have to ask yourself, 'Do I want to be like that again?' Because there is no middle ground, you won't be able to moderate and will end right back up at square one.

Unfortunately, this is easier said than done and many of us slip up. I did. But you know what? There is absolutely nothing wrong with slipping up. In fact, for me it was probably what led to me quitting completely. It reaffirmed the fact that I could not drink in moderation, it reiterated that I had a major problem. It was a short (three month) reminder that drink, drugs and I simply could not work together.

You will have good days and bad, but always remember that a bad day when you're sober is 100 times better than a bad day when you're using drink or drugs.

It's perfectly OK to slip up. There is nothing to be ashamed of. The mere fact that you've slipped up means that you've had some time sober and that is something to be incredibly proud of. I have all the respect in the world for someone who never gives up trying to get sober but has had a slip from time to time. This is far better than someone who has just never tried giving up and admits defeat without doing the work.

If you do slip up, you mustn't condemn yourself to being a failure – you're not. The fact is, you've probably been addicted to something for many years and stopping that is such a massive change in behaviour that there will be times when you are tested.

Very few people get it right the first time. It's about learning from your mistakes.

When I had my setback, I hadn't made the right decision. I'd gone for the 'I'll stop drinking for a while, prove to everyone that I don't have a problem and then see what happens' option. In my mind I knew that I wasn't ready to give up and I inevitably slipped up.

If you do fall down, get back up and go again. Read more, speak to people if you need, tell them why you started drinking or taking drugs again. Check out YouTube, there are many stories of those who took multiple attempts to stop. It is normal. You've been married to your drug of choice and even though you're separated, you will still think of them. You know getting back together would never work, but desire does funny things. We all make mistakes.

No one will blame you for slipping up (well, apart from yourself). This is probably the hardest thing as the feelings of self-loathing and hate will come flooding back. If this happens, use them to your advantage, this helped me greatly. I got to the point where I'd tasted sobriety and had experienced going back. I fucking knew sobriety was better; I'd experienced it, lived it and knew it was the only way for me to live. Even if you only manage two days sober before slipping up, if you can get some time under your belt you will have felt that feeling of waking up and being 100 percent you. Tell yourself that's how you want to feel every day, because the simple fact is, you can!

Whatever happens, be proud, please be proud of every day of sobriety you achieve. Everyone around you will be proud of you. But as I have said throughout this book, it's all about you. Tell yourself that every day, have a big fucking smirk on your face as you know that you're sober and you've done something superhuman. You are a superhero, you really are.

It's OK to still think about drink and drugs even when you're sober; it's normal. If you slip up, that's OK too, but never give up giving up.

Clare Pooley, who I've cited before regarding her must-watch Ted Talk 'Making sober less shameful' finishes by saying, 'There is no shame in being sober, only joy and pride and freedom.' I could not agree more with these words.

CHAPTER 6

Help Others

The sole purpose of me writing this book is to help you. I have lived the ups, I have experienced the downs, I have been the addict and now I am sober.

This story can be yours too, and I hope many of you reading this will be able to put pen to paper and share your journey. You see the one thing about every successful sober story is that it always has a happy ending.

People will occasionally try and tell you otherwise, but they are the ones whose stories no one would be interested in reading. There's a sad reality to all this, which is many people won't get sober. It's a lifestyle and behavioural change that requires routine and work. But it is doable if you follow the structure I've laid out and, most importantly, if you yourself want to get sober.

Whilst this journey is about you, it's not one you can take alone. Many people have helped me on my way, some of those people don't even know that they did, but it doesn't matter, the help is out there, and I got it. You can get it too.

I'm now in a place where I feel completely confident I will never pick up a drink or take drugs again, no matter what happens. Therefore, I felt it was my time to help others.

You see, when you conquer something, you want to talk about it. Imagine if those first pioneers of Everest were asked to share their stories and they simply said, 'Nah I don't really want to talk about it.' Nothing would be learnt, and it wouldn't help those who followed in their path.

I hope that sharing my story has helped you reach your decision. Maybe you've already made it, or perhaps you've been sober for years. Whatever your situation might be, I hope that by passing on the information I've learnt, the experiences I've been through, my view on drink and drugs and the mess I got myself into (and eventually out of), I'll help you on your path to sobriety.

I believe part of my experience, in fact my duty, is to guide others. If I can help just one person change their life, then I will have succeeded.

I'm not alone, there are many of us out there sharing our stories – go and read them all if you need. I guarantee you this, once you have gone through it yourself, you too will want to share your new life with others, and I encourage you to do so.

I would love to hear your stories too as this journey is one that keeps on giving. I still read about sobriety, I still watch the videos and I'm now very proud to have shared my story with you in my own honest way.

The sober community is one filled only with love, compassion, pride and heroic accounts. I think I can speak for all authors, vloggers, podcasters, doctors, drug and alcohol support staff, whoever it may be, that they are united in their mission. It's very simple – help others.

What Good Has Come From Me Getting Sober?

Before I provide my final thoughts, I want to share my personal list of the good things that have come from getting sober. You may feel that some of these items are a bit pretentious, but I don't care, it's my list. When you write yours, I won't judge it, I'll just smile from ear to ear thinking, 'well done, well done, well done'.

- I have regained my wife and family's trust
- I have regained my self-respect
- I have better relationships with everyone in my life
- I now lead by example
- I spend much more time with my children
- I make good decisions. They may not always be right, but I know that they were made with a completely clear head
- I have lost twenty kilos in weight
- I sleep well every night
- I look better
- I have improved my work and productivity
- I have bought a flat in Paris
- I have bought a new car
- I have saved money for the first time in my life
- I have invested money for the first time in my life

- I am fitter than I have ever been
- I appreciate the mornings, every morning
- I no longer fear Mondays
- I have read thirty-eight books and counting
- I have taken my daughter and son to a Formula 1 Grand Prix race
- I know who my real friends are
- I have more time
- I feel proud of myself
- I look forward to the future
- I have written a book to help others achieve the same things

I also compiled a list of all the good things that came from being addicted to drink and drugs, here it is:

Time to Recap

No one said getting sober was going to be easy, but the reality is it's also not that hard. The arseholes of the world would say, just stop doing what you're doing. You and I know it doesn't work like that, but once you've made your decision and built your plan with all the support structure you require, it can be simple.

The one thing that I can guarantee you is this is the best decision you will ever make in your life. Everything gets better when you get sober. Everything.

Embrace it, look at yourself as unique, because you are. You've been to hell, had a mooch around and decided it's not for you. You've decided to do something that is truly life changing.

People talk about life-changing events – winning money, getting married, having kids, a new job. But I can tell you this, nothing, absolutely nothing will alter your life more than getting sober.

You can finally be the person you want to be: that proud, happy person that you know exists deep down.

For so many years I had dreams that never materialised because I was too busy talking about them whilst drunk or high. Pointless talk with no action. Getting sober has changed all that.

You can do it too. Even if at first you don't succeed, try, try and try again. There is a French proverb that says, *Il n'y a que celui qui ne fait rien qui ne se trompe jamais.* It translates as, 'Only a person that does nothing never makes any mistakes.' Think about that. If you are doing something about the situation you're in and you make mistakes, it doesn't matter. Keep doing something about it. Never give up giving up.

I truly believe that if you want to change and follow these steps, you can get sober and stay that way. What I know for sure is that it worked for me. I wrote this book to help you and I hope it has. And from the bottom of my heart, I would like to thank you for having taken the time to read it. This book is part of my journey and if I can be part of yours then I have achieved what I set out to.

So, to recap:

Make your decision – do you really want to change?

Decide if you need professional help.

Create your plan – fill your time, have projects.

Tell people (or not) – you decide.

Prepare your elevator speech – plan how to deal with the questions.

Do the work – read and watch. Constantly.

Get into exercise.

Stay sober – don't worry about slipping up.

Never give up giving up.

Help others.

Be proud.

Be sober.

Welcome to your new life. You're going to love it.

Printed in Great Britain
by Amazon